HARD MEN AND JELLY BABIES

To: MARGARET / COLIN.

Lots of Love

Hard Men and Jelly Babies
Copyright © Don Smith 2007

ISBN 9781-84426-413-1

First Published 2007 by
UPFRONT PUBLISHING LTD
Peterborough, England.

XX

Printed by Printondemand-Worldwide Ltd.

Don Smith was born in the cotton-manufacturing town of Bolton, in the County of Lancashire in 1933.

He received a secondary modern school education.

He was an all round athlete, participating at soccer, boxing and swimming.

On leaving school, at 15, he became an apprentice joiner to a Mr R G Hurst and Sons. In 1952, he married Jean; when they were both 18 years of age. Their first son was born later the same year. At 19 years of age he was called-up for National Service, he later signed-on as a regular soldier for the extra pay. He served in West Germany, Italy, Korea, Japan and Malaya.

At the age of 22, he held the rank of (acting) sergeant in the King's Regiment.

In 1964 he joined Her Majesty's Prison Service and served at HM Prison Stangeways, Buckley Hall Detention Centre, Aylesbury (Young Prisoner's Prison), HM Prison Wandsworth and finally ending his service at HM Prison Parkhurst on the Isle of Wight

He now resides on the Isle of Wight with his *original* wife Jean. They have six children, 17 grandchildren, and four great-grandchildren. He retired in 1990. He enjoys a daily swim, bird watching, fishing and an occasional round of golf.

Together, they spend the winter months in the beautiful country of The Gambia in West Africa.

Hard Men and Jelly Babies

DON SMITH

UPFRONT PUBLISHING
PETERBOROUGH, ENGLAND

Acknowledgements

I am indebted to my wife Jean for her tolerance and understanding; also my children David, Don, Donna, Sue, Barbara and Duncan, just for being themselves. Any shortcomings are my own responsibility.

Chapter 1
In the Beginning

When you decide to write the story of your life, it must be best to start at the beginning. Someone else once wrote: 'in the beginning…'

The day I came into this world was 6 April 1933. At about this time big changes were taking place in Germany. Very few people were aware what the consequences would be of Adolf Hitler's rise to fame. At that time I knew nothing about the dangerous situation that was pending in Germany; my main concern was awaiting my mother's breasts to appear at regular intervals.

My first recollection of life was, when aged about eighteen months old, being bitten by a black dog whilst holding my tiny hand out to stroke the hound.

I was born in Bolton District General Hospital, in the cotton mill Town of Bolton - Lancashire. I was the first child of Fred and Alice Smith. Fredrick Victor Smith, my father, was a regular soldier. He was a nasty man, who always smelled of beer and would always be beating my mother, for reasons I did not understand at that time. I now know that he was a sadist and a bully.

When he was on leave from the army our life was miserable and fearful. Never in all my life did my father show me any affection. Never did he buy me sweets or Christmas presents. Any gifts I received were from my mother, who over many years was to become the best, most caring mother that anyone could wish for. In 1935, my sister Barbara was born. How happy I was to have a playmate. I was very proud of my baby sister and loved her very much.

With the Second World War about to commence, we saw less and less of our Fred Smith father; when he was away ours was a very happy home. Mother took in washing and ironing to make ends meet. My mother's mother (grandma Moores) was always there to help us out.

She was a very kindly person, very religious, and was always singing psalms and hymns. I once remember her giving a dirty-looking man a six-penny piece.

He said, "How kind of you my dear, but I am a coal miner." He then handed the coin back to grandma.

When Barbara and I were old enough, Grandma Moores used to baby sit, whilst our mother worked in the cotton mills. We started to prosper; new chairs, linoleum, and a new hand-made rug to cover the bare stone flags, which once were the floor. Occasionally Fred Smith would appear on the scene, home on leave, how I used to dread those times. More beatings for my mother, and grandma was far too scared to hang around. Fred Smith was a big man, an alcoholic and a bully, and when I said my prayers at bedtime, I did pray that a German would shoot him; such was my hatred and fear of him. His beating of my mother had to be stopped. It broke my heart to see her bruised and always cowering away from this thug. I vowed I would kill him when I was big enough. The thought of a child yes! But I was sincere.

My sister and I used to sleep together under the stairs, or in the Anderson air raid shelter in the garden. We both preferred to be under the stairs, because it was warm and not damp like the shelter was out in the garden. But when the air raids where heavy, our mother would always tuck us up together in the air raid shelter. We found it all very exciting, but on reflection, they were very dangerous times.

We still had to attend school and mother had to go to work in that awful cotton mill. She once took me to have a look round the mill and said, "One day you will be here son."

I thought, even at that young age, that the cotton mill was not going to be my future employment.

The smell and heat put me off from the start; anyway I fancied a job in the open air.

We lived on the edge of the town and just across from our house we could always see the cows in the field. About one mile away was the start of the moorland and the vast expanse of the Pennine hills.

This area was my kingdom, my playing fields. My best pal was Norman Berry. We would wander over those hills for miles, seeking plover birds' eggs to supplement our meagre wartime rations. Even lapwing or curlews' eggs were fair game. I once remember cooking a moorhen on a log fire, not much to eat and not very nice.

The tricks we used to get up to. Half the golf course had been cultivated; crops of sugar beet and turnip had been planted, as well as our favourite Brussels sprouts. The farmer always planted his potato crop very close to his farmhouse; he knew that they were top of our menu.

Yet under the cover of darkness, we always managed a couple of sacks a week. His foreman, George, would trade them off for golf balls that we found in the wheat fields. Everyone was encouraged to have an allotment.

And despite the war, we always had the fruit and vegetable competitions.

Old Mr Hamer always appeared to win everything, we found out later that he had amassed a great pile of horse manure before the war and it was now proving to be his 'secret weapon'. I look back and feel that the war did not do us any great harm. I was never hungry; people got on with their lives and made the best of a bad job. Sadly, the bombing killed many, especially in the Manchester area.

Mother was now working more overtime to make up for the times that they had to rush from the mill to the air raid shelters; shelters were everywhere. In the schools and built at irregular intervals in the places where most people were congregated. Toward the end of the war, when the allies were gaining the upper hand, the air raids became less frequent and eventually by 1944 they stopped altogether.

Barbara and I spent the whole of the war either under the stairs and or in the shelter, mother would never take the slightest risk with us. All this love and attention and working a sixty hour week in the cotton mill, she was a wonderful mother, pity about our father. Thankfully he found himself another woman and went to live in the Newcastle area.

It was just after the war that mother started to build us a proper home. Out went the greatcoats off the beds and the handmade rugs were replaced by shining linoleum, modest yes! At the time it was a wonderful transformation. I was twelve years of age now; Barbara was ten years old. I had a daily paper round, delivering newspapers mornings and evenings. At weekends, I helped Jack Simm on his farm. He was a stingy old man, but his wife Kitty always gave me a good dinner and a dozen cracked eggs to take home. She was a kindly woman, who having no children of her own used to spoil me. I think she would have adopted me if my mother had allowed it. Good old Kitty Simm, I shall never forget her kindness.

1946 and still no sign of food rationing being ended, we did not know it at the time but it would be another five years before clothing and food rationing would end. At school, I was never the top of the class and never at the bottom. But I was good at all types of sport and in this I thought my future lay.

I left school in 1948 and my mother insisted that I become an apprentice joiner. Mother found me a job in a little shop that made furniture. The owner was a big fat man, named Bill Morris. He had two grown-up sons, both in their middle to late twenties.

Both were like their father, very fat and bullies. I was just the tea-lad and was used for all the menial tasks; I could spend days on end rubbing a sideboard down with different grades of sandpaper.

I was very unhappy because my half-day off was Wednesday, to fit in with the owner's weekly game of golf. I had to work all day Saturday; that meant playing soccer was out. Mr Morris was the stingiest man I have ever known, he even deducted tea and sugar payments from my meagre wage of eleven shillings a week - that is equal to 55 pence in today's money. I told my mother that I was being bullied and that I was very unhappy. My mother went to see Mr Morris and gave him a piece of her mind. In the meantime, I had obtained a place on an Apprenticeship Scheme. This scheme was run by the Council to promote apprenticeships. We worked under skilled instructors, building actual houses. Potential employers would visit the unit and select a lad of their choice. I had been fixing door casings and skirting boards for about three months when one day I was called into the office and introduced to a mister Stanley Hirst.

Mr Hirst was the owner of a very reputable joinery firm in the town. He asked me several questions then said, "You start on Monday at eight o'clock, don't be late."

My new boss appeared to be a very nice man and over the next three years proved to be so. He had a workforce of about twenty, plus two apprentices; I was the youngest and therefore started learning the skills later. We all got on very well together. Mr Hirst had formulated a system which allowed you to work with a different joiner for a few months at a time, thereby getting to know various skills and techniques; it also allowed you to get to know different types of men. Some had come straight out of the services, most having seen active service.

Looking back, I find it strange that not one of them ever told you of their exploits during the war. I did like working with a man named Bob Tatlock. He was always happy and full of fun, yet was a very skilled joiner. He was always given the prestige work at the breweries or the public houses. That meant a free pint at lunchtime. Bob had no children and children were out of the question. I found out later that whilst a prisoner of war he had been castrated by the Japanese, all for trying to escape. Bob was my idol, he worked hard and passed on his skills to me at all times, and he always called a 'spade a spade'. As part of the rules of my apprenticeship, I had to attend night school and one day a week I attended 'day-release' at the technical college; this commitment was very difficult for me to maintain. I was far too interested in sport, and had recently met Jean my girlfriend. I was besotted with her and I just wanted to be with her as often as I could.

My work at college suffered and the head of the school reported my poor attendance and progress to my employer. He was sympathetic, but told me clearly that if I did not attend night school and improve my grades he would rescind my apprenticeship. He said I was going to ruin my chance of a good steady, skilled occupation, and that I would finish up on the shit pile. He was right, but at that age, I thought I knew better than anyone did.

I had the thought of National Service on my mind. I knew that if I gave up the apprenticeship I would be called-up for National Service within weeks. I spoke to Jean and decided to finish my apprenticeship, go into the army and get the two years serving the Queen and Country over and done with.

On 15 March 1952, Jean and I were married. We were both eighteen, and at the altar, we were not alone. Jean was pregnant, carrying our son David. In June 1952, I was called up into the army.

I had first met Jean three years before we were married. I was looking out of my window when I saw John McGuiness, a mate of mine, walking past my house with this beautiful girl by his side. It was love at first sight. I said to myself, "I will make that girl mine."

A few days later I was walking out in the countryside with my girlfriend Dorothy. Walking toward us were John McGuiness and this lovely looking girl. We met, and started to talk. I asked the girl what her name was.

"Jean," she replied.

I said, "Jean, I would like you to start coming out with me."

Jean said that she was with John. I said he would not mind if she came with me. John never said a word; poor Dorothy who was not at all that keen on going out with me said nothing. So, Jean and I took our first walk together.

Later Jean said, "If John had complained I would not have left him for you."

That happened 57 years ago. Jean has been my wife for 54 years now. Over that long period, we have had good times and bad times, sadness and happiness. We had six children, three boys and three girls, and at this time (2006) we have seventeen grandchildren and four great-grandchildren.

Sadly, our eldest son David died in 2003 aged 51. He was a grandfather himself and his death was the most tragic event that had occurred in the whole of our lifetime.

Back to 1952, my apprenticeship was annulled and it was only a few weeks before I found myself called-up for National Service. Two years of my life and that of my family, given up for Queen and Country, well that is how it was said at the time; it was in fact conscription dressed up in a more acceptable way; it was off to war. I had to report to the headquarters of the Loyal North Lancashire Regiment, which was located at Fullwood barracks in the City of Lancaster.

As I entered the old barracks gate, a soldier shouted, "Get your hands out of your pockets you little shit!" Oh dear! I thought, 'I am in for a rough time here.' There were about 120 new recruits, most were conscripted National Service members, but there were a few men who had signed-on as regular soldiers; some for as long as 22 years.

We were housed in dormitory type huts, and then we were all marched off to be issued with our uniform, rifle, and other essential items of kit. Later that day we met the Commanding Officer, who read us all the riot act, and told us that he had made soldiers out of lesser men than us. A saying that he obviously used on every new intake, he then gave us a brief history of the regiment, telling us that his infantry soldiers were the best in the world. He also told us that we would be confined to barracks for the six weeks of our basic training. That made me feel homesick straight from the off. I was already missing my wife and I had only just arrived.

The bugle woke you up and told you when to go to sleep. After a full day marching, doing weapon training and seeing how many times you could march round the parade ground before you dropped, you were ready for bed well before the bugler played the 'last post'. I do not think that during that 'six weeks from hell' I never once heard the last post. The training was hard and very demanding, each day your body became more accustomed to the exercise, and it became easier. We all became fitter and after the six weeks training, I was as fit as I had ever been in my life, but that was just the start.

On reflection the six weeks passed very quickly and finally it was the day of the passing-out parade. Our family could come to watch the parade by kind invitation of the Commanding Officer.

My Jeanie and my mother and new stepfather attended. I was so proud at that time, because I had put everything into the training; I had done better than most in all aspects of the training. Modestly, I can record that I was selected the best recruit on that intake.

After a meeting with our loved ones for the first time in six weeks we had tea and cake and we were all given a 48 hour pass to go home. How I enjoyed those hours with Jeanie. I did not want to go back but I was fully aware of the consequences if I did not. Had I known the future I just may not have returned.

On returning to Fullwood, we were told that we were to be sent to Trieste in Northern Italy. No leave, no goodbyes, nothing! On reflection, they treated us like cattle. I telephoned Jeanie and she was heartbroken. She was about six months pregnant. I asked the Commanding Officer for special compassionate leave but my request was refused. I was very unhappy by his heartless decision. Ah well! Grin and bear it, but it did leave a bitter taste. So, it was off to Trieste. I had never been out of the UK before so going through Holland and over the Alps was an experience.

Being in the British infantry is not unlike going back to basic training again. You are introduced to new weapons and various weapons of destruction. Grenades of various sizes and shapes, the Bren and Sten gun, the Browning and Lewis machine guns, all of them great effective weapons. We would practise stripping down these guns until we knew them all as well as we knew the back of our hands. Every other day we would be out on the firing ranges for target practice; then it would be weapon cleaning and theory. In between all that activity we would be marching and counter marching. Without being conceited, we were a very efficient regiment. Every Saturday and Sunday the routine was more relaxed and we could take part in sporting activities.

I had always been a keen soccer player and boxer and it was not long before I was representing the battalion at both soccer and boxing. I fought as a middleweight (maximum eleven stone seven pounds) all the time I was in the army. I could maintain this weight by exercise and the correct diet. Athletes and sportsmen generally, are encouraged in their respective sports and received the best coaching and extra food to keep them in trim. It was whilst in Trieste that I played in the same Brigade football team as Sir Bobby Robson. Bobby was inside right and I was centre forward. We played a team representing the Italian police and we won 2-0. I shall never forget that game because I had a stinker, I shall always remember Bobby Robson saying to me in the bath, "We would have had a dozen goals but for you."

He had some nerve saying that to the brigade middleweight boxing champion. Maybe he did not know that fact. Anyway, what he did say was correct; I had played a very poor game. Ironically, I had scored seven goals in a previous game I had played, against an Austrian XI. Bobby was not there to see me score all those goals, because being a semi-professional footballer had been flown home to play for his club, Ipswich Town. I do not believe that Robson was ever sent abroad again.

Everyone now knows just how well his distinguished career went from there. He played soccer for England and many prominent clubs.

He later became the head coach of the England team and finished his career as manager of Newcastle United. He was aged 71 when he retired from Newcastle, yet still found time to appear on many TV and radio programmes. In 2000, Bobby Robson became Sir Bobby Robson, knighted for his services to soccer, an honour which was very well deserved. I still follow his career with great interest. Other army soccer players I had played with whilst in the army, who became professionals, were Jimmy Armfield (Blackpool) and Jimmy Meadows (Manchester City).

I was only married to Jeanie in March of 1952. I joined the army in June 1952 and arrived back in the UK in August 1955. At last, home from Korea and the Far East, a tour of duty that had lasted for over two and a half years. I had signed on as a regular soldier, not out of patriotism, but for the extra cash, so I only had myself to blame for the separation from my wife and son. I had been away since 1952 and since that time had been stationed in Germany, Austria, and Trieste in Northeast Italy. So, in that short period we had spent only a few weeks together, far too long a parting. Well, I was now returning to my home and the homesickness was well behind me.

From the boat at Liverpool we were taken to Lancaster barracks by rail and de-mobbed. It was a great feeling to board the train and head for Bolton, a taxi to our little terraced house in Spa Road, very near to the gasworks, and there waiting outside the gate in the autumn sunshine was Jeanie and our little son David. I was a very happy man.

Jeanie and I soon started where we had left off. I had been in love with Jeanie since she was fifteen, from the very first time I saw her walking past my home, with her first boyfriend John McGuiness; I knew she was the girl for me. I was a big-headed bully in those days. If the army had done nothing else, it had made me much more mature and far more responsible.

The army life had made me lazy and unsettled. When I was discharged, I had held the rank of acting sergeant, a most notable achievement for a young man of 22. After several years at trying to find a suitable job, I became very depressed. I seemed to be getting nowhere.

By 1960 I had been a miner, plasterer's labourer and farmhand and had worked in a plastics factory, working twelve-hour shifts.

Three more children had arrived, Donald, Donna and Susan. I had to earn more, but I still thought I was Sergeant Smith and that the world owed me a living. I was not being a good husband or father. I had to change direction; I was not content, changing jobs every few months. I did work hard, but my aggressive attitude lost me friends and jobs. Thank God Jeanie put up with me. We were re-housed on medical grounds; young Donald had developed continual chest infections, caused by living too close to the gasworks and the railway. We went back to live in the north of Bolton, close to Moss Bank Park, very close to where Jean and I had originated from before getting married.

One evening whilst decorating one of the bedrooms I came across an application form to join Her Majesty's Prison Service. The previous tenant had left it in a chest of drawers. This I thought was just what I was looking for.

Not the army, no more separation from my family, but a job I knew I could take to and enjoy. I had to try it, a job that offered a future for all of us.

Later that evening Jeanie and I talked about my wish to join HM Prison service. I do not think she fancied the idea. Next day I spoke to my parents.

My stepfather's response, "Do what you bloody well want; you can't do any worse than you are doing at the moment."

My mother was against it. I had always been her little boy. She had always wanted to protect me. My stepfather did not know about any of the troubles my mother had saved me from. As a boy, I had stolen a neighbour's engagement ring and given it to my mother, because she did not have one. During the war, I had stolen boxes of jam from a broken down lorry. I had hidden the jam in a cave in a quarry and brought a jar home every week, telling my mother that a man gave me the jam for doing odd jobs for him. I can never remember being without jam during the war. I also stole a duck from the park for Christmas dinner because we had nothing to eat.

I was only taken to court once, for causing some damage to trees. I was fined twelve shillings and sixpence (63p in today's money), with seven shillings and six pence costs. The trees were for firewood to keep us warm, how times have changed. I remember my mother crying in court and telling the magistrate what a good little boy I was. What a perfect future candidate for Her Majesty's Prison Service. I had to be 'up front' on the application form so I declared all my past crimes and posted it off.

Chapter 2
Off to the Land of the Morning Calm - Korea

I had just finished breakfast when I was ordered to meet with the CO (Commanding Officer.) My first thoughts were to think that something could have happened to Jean or my baby son.

I knocked on the CO's door and was admitted at once.

"Good news Smith, you are going back home," the CO said.

I asked if my family was OK.

"Yes! Your family is well. You are one of twenty soldiers, who are going back to the UK to form part of the new King's Own Regiment, who are due to go to the Far East. I am sorry that I cannot give you any more information, only that you will be able to spend some time with your family before you set sail."

I was over the moon at the time, because at least I would get to see my wife and son. I was so excited and I could not sleep that night. I could not understand the implications of my sudden transfer at that time.

Next day I met the other soldiers who were returning to the UK. All of them were the scum of the regiment; all had been in trouble. 'The Commanding Officer is getting rid of the dead wood,' I thought to myself. 'What had I ever done to be placed in the same class as these reprobates?'

My mind went back to a few months previously, when six of us were ordered to carry out duties at the British Embassy. We had all been issued with white gloves, and we were taken to the embassy in the centre of Trieste. We all alighted from the transport and were ordered to put on the white gloves.

The sergeant said, "You are all car park attendants this evening, get organised and do not forget your manners."

I thought for a few minutes and I said to the sergeant, "Sorry sarge but I am not being a car park attendant, I joined the army, not the highway patrol."

"It is an order! Are you refusing to obey my orders?" the sergeant bawled.

"Yes!" I said.

I was escorted back to barracks and located in the guardroom. Next day I received 28 days confined to camp, along with the usual punishment that went with it. So this must be the reason I am being sent back to the UK. With Jean and my son on my mind, I could not care a toss. This, refusing an order, had been the only time in all my service that I had been up before the CO. Fortunately, I was never again ordered to wear white gloves.

Chapter 3
Over the Alps – Heading Back Home

S ix thick slices of bread, a few ounces of cheese and an apple; this was to be my food supply until we arrived back in the UK.

We did have our water bottles, full to the brim.

Because there had been a roof fall in one of the rail tunnels, we had to travel home in a coach. It would take us about eighteen hours to get to the UK so I was not looking forward to this long trip.

As we left Trieste, we started to climb up into the foothills of the Italian Alps. Steeper and more precarious, looking into those ravines made your tummy turn. After three hours we crossed the Italian/Austrian border, yet more and more steeper mountains, scary bends and sheer drops into the abyss. I was glad when night-time came then, at least I could not see the potential dangers.

As we entered West Germany, I started to think more and more of Jean and my young son. We had now left the mountains and snow behind us, the sun rose in the East; you could see that the world was flat again.

We arrived in Holland about twelve hours after our departure. The bread and cheese had long gone and I was starving. We boarded the ship 'HMT Vienna' (Her Majesty's Transport Ship) at the port of the Hook of Holland; the ship would take us to Harwich. A train to

Formby in Lancashire and something to eat I hope. They say that an army marches on its stomach, good job I did not have to march.

Chapter 4
Harrington Barracks, Formby
- Lancs.

We arrived at Harrington barracks, and the first thing I needed was something to eat. It had been a very long and tiring journey and I soon found my way to the cookhouse.

The barracks were simply lots of wooden huts and large canvas marquees; just the administration block was an actual brick building.

I asked the platoon commander if I could get some leave to go and visit my wife and son, it had been months since I last saw them. The platoon commander sanctioned my leave, a 36 hour pass. I thought to myself, 'The generous bastard!' Ah well! It was Bolton here I come, so be thankful for small mercies.

I arrived at my mother-in-law's home, where my wife and son were living. I entered the house. Jean's sister told me that Jean was in hospital and was suffering from pneumonia. I felt as sick as a parrot. Why had no one informed me sooner? I visited the hospital at once, but alas, poor Jean was far too poorly to talk to me. I gave her a cuddle and a kiss and I said to myself that I had to do something to see my sick wife more often.

I could not concentrate on being a soldier. I returned home and saw David my son; he was now close on nine months old, he did not know me from Adam.

Next day I returned to barracks and went to see my CO. I told him of my wife's ill heath, he appeared very sympathetic. The sergeant who was also present came out with a very snide remark, "Trying to dodge the trip abroad Smith?"

I had not even thought of where we were being sent to, however, I could have, at a guess, known that it was nowhere in the UK. The CO gave me seven days' leave and wished my wife a speedy recovery. I was off like a shot.

I spent the next seven days at the bedside of my wife; she was very poorly and further complications had set in.

The seven days' leave flew past.

I returned to the barracks, heavy of heart and with no interest whatsoever in the army.

I saw one of my mates, who said to me, "We are off to Korea in three weeks' time."

Christ! That is all I needed.

That evening, everyone was excited at the prospect of sailing 13,000 miles to the other side of the world; I did not share this happiness. Jean's health was like a millstone around my neck, I could not think of anything else.

I had to inform the CO regarding my worry. On the way to his office, I met the sergeant who had previously accused me of swinging the lead. As I passed him, he said, "Smith, you are just after getting out of going to Korea. Are you chicken?"

This remark stopped me in my tracks.
Yes! Everyone will think that I am dodging the draft. I went to the NAAFI and telephoned the hospital, to inquire about my wife. The nurse informed me that Jean was a little better. This news cheered me up somewhat.

Next day I went to see the CO, and again made a request for compassionate leave. I was given a 36 hour pass; 'better than nothing,' I thought.

My CO was an officer and a gentleman. However, the sergeant had made a valid point, one which I had to ponder.

Had I known what I do now? I would never have sailed to Korea, I would have gone AWOL. Then, if I was apprehended and sent to an army jail, how would I ever see my family again?

I was to be away from my family for two and a half years, I did not know this at the time, but on reflection, it was a punishment that I did not deserve.

I made the decision to go to Korea with the minimum of fuss, get it over with, and not be a chicken, bloody fool that I was.

Jean was on the mend, so it did make my departure a little easier, but how I was homesick, and I had not even boarded the ship yet. I said my goodbyes to Jean and my son, and I had to make the best of a bad job. This I did and I soon became a more mature person and a better soldier.

Well, it was off to the land of the morning calm.

Chapter 5
The Long Voyage

After a sad farewell we departed by train to Southampton, there we embarked on the ship HMT Fowey.

It was a very large ship, carrying over a thousand troops, plus the crew. A military band played us off and everyone appeared to be in good spirits. We enjoyed a good meal and if this was a taste of things to come, I could...

We soon sailed past the Channel Isles, and it was not long before we were crossing the Bay of Biscay. I had heard tales of storms and gales, but on this occasion the sea was as calm as a millpond. A few more days and we headed through the Straits of Gibraltar. It was dark and we could see the lights in the North African country of Morocco, it was a wonderful sight.

A week out and everything changed; we had been given a week to find our sea legs, and now it was time to get fit and get used to our weapons. The rifle, Bren and Lewis machine guns.

We also had to get into tip-top physical shape; I can assure you the instructors knew their job.

After two more weeks we were fitter than fiddles. I could re-assemble a Bren gun in the dark and my rifle was now a part of me; all the pokey drill (drill and exercise using your rifle) had paid off.

At Cyprus, we pulled into Larnica to transfer a soldier to the hospital on the island. No troops were allowed to get off the ship, probably because Cyprus looked so tranquil and beautiful that many would have done a runner. Not for me, I had written over a dozen letters to Jean and some to my parents, I posted the letters, knowing full well that they would be sent on to the UK from Cyprus.

Next day we had sight of Egypt, we were heading for the entrance to the Suez Canal at Port Said; it was a very exciting time, the decks were crowded with troops, all taking in the wonderful views. We passed through lock after lock, and we reached the port of Suez in about ten hours. It was now night-time and there were not many lights on the banks of the canal, however, it was still very hot. We were informed that during the day the temperature and reached fifty degrees centigrade, far too hot for comfort. It was still very hot under the stars, what a beautiful sight.

Next day we reached Aden, in the country of The Yemen, which is located on the South of the Arabian Peninsular.

Finally, some of us were allowed shore leave. Coaches had been laid on; we all sped off to a seaside town, which had an open-air swimming pool. The only trouble was it was far too hot to walk on the tiles, so we had to use our boots to make it to the pool.

Lads will be lads, and some boots were soon floating on the pool surface. Then back to the ship and a big plate of eggs and chips, with lots of freshly-baked bread.

As we sailed into the Red Sea, I could see the steep, very high, red cliffs of Ethiopia; they appeared to extend forever. Darkness fell and we were soon entering the

Indian Ocean. Since reaching Suez, I had opted to sleep on deck under the stars; I still cannot get used to a bloody hammock.

Two days into the Indian Ocean and the sea became much choppier, the wind was getting stronger. In the evening, the film *The Great Caruso* was showing in the ship's theatre.

I went to the theatre early to get a favourable seat; the theatre was full to near capacity by the time I arrived. It was noticeable that the storm was becoming more severe, the ship was rolling and the wind could be heard over the soundtrack of the film.

You could not hear Mario singing; it was as if he was just miming.

The storm lasted over six hours; many passengers were very seasick, several had received minor injuries caused by falls. After the storm, our evening meal was delayed, because the storm had caused damage in the kitchen; we were informed that one cook had been scalded.

The Fowey was not a small ship, had it been smaller I firmly believe that damage could have been far more serious.

The ship sailed on towards our next port of call, Colombo.

During this time we continued with our vigorous training schedule, we were as physically fit as was possible. During the voyage many of us had qualified for marksmen on the rifle and Bren gun. Apart from wearing the marksman's badges on your uniform sleeve, it would mean an extra shilling a week on your pay.

We entered the port of Colombo, the capital of Ceylon (now Sri Lanka). We had been promised shore leave, but at the last minute, it was decided that to catch the high tide, we would just take on some water and get on our way. I made sure that my pile of letters arrived at the purser's office in good time, ready to be posted.

Ceylon was the furthest South we had come. It was very hot, but in no way hotter than in the Red Sea and it was very lush, with vegetation and lovely palms. We were still in full training; it had all become a routine task to us all.

Now we were heading further south, next port of call Singapore in Malaya (the furthest South that we would travel).

Singapore is just 85 miles north of the equator. After that, we would be heading north, up to China and the British Colony of Hong Kong. Alas, no crossing the equator ceremony.

During a shooting practice the Tannoy system came on and our CO said that he had an important announcement to make. I thought to myself, 'I bet the Queen is expecting.' How wrong I was.

The CO said, "Officers and other ranks, the war in Korea has ended, I will give you all more details later."

Well! That was a bolt out of the blue; no one had ever mentioned the fighting in Korea. I think everyone thought it was taboo, but I had detected that the nearer we had been to our destination everyone appeared to write home more. 27 July 1953 was the day I thought I would now be certain of getting back to my family in one piece.

Would it now make my separation from my wife shorter? I would very much like to think so. Ah well! Just how wrong can you be? All I could now think of was getting to Korea and getting out as soon as I could.

Although we had been informed that a peace treaty was to be signed by the UN we continued with our vigorous training. If anything, I felt it had become more intense.

Apart from being homesick I must admit that I enjoyed the wonderful sights we were seeing, and we were very well looked after by the crew of the ship, in particular the food.

Just over halfway and heading for Hong Kong. It was still a Crown Colony in those days; now it is part of the Republic of China. A week later and we entered Hong Kong harbour, which can boast 235 islands; I was rather surprised to see all the junks and sampans, hundreds of them. Most of these boats were home, not just for the crew, but all their families and their livestock as well.

Again, I made sure I posted all my mail, this time I confirmed in writing that the Korean War was ended. However, I am sure my wife and parents would have picked up the news in the media.

No shore leaves again; the officers were becoming concerned that there could be a mass exodus of troops. Next stop Korea.

The weather was still very warm and the dolphins were still following the ship. One chap thought they were the same dolphins that had been following us when in the Med. weeks before. A ship's crewmember told me that the dolphins followed the boat because they thought the ship was their mother. What a nice thought. The flying fish were still with us; what people do not realise is that the fish only fly to escape from predators. It was still very hot and I was still sleeping on deck; I could never get used to those hammocks.

Late in August, we arrived at the Port of Pusan on the southern coast of South Korea. My first impression of Korea was not favourable. The docks and the surrounding area were grimy looking and there was a great deal of damage to the buildings, there was also a foul smell.

Well! Chin, chin and make the best of a bad job; we remained on the ship until next day. We then disembarked in an orderly British fashion. We left the ship in order of Companies – A-B-C… Along the dockside was the biggest row of tables I had ever seen. We were issued with another kitbag and issued with all our winter clothing and footwear. A great big parka jacket, woollen socks, long johns, thick woollen hats, wire mesh insoles and balaclavas.

Considering the temperature was now in the upper eighties it appeared strange to be issued with all this Arctic gear. Off to the North Pole, perhaps! In a few months time I would soon appreciate these winter extras.

After being issued with the new kit, we boarded trains to take us north to the capital Seoul.

Whilst on this long voyage I had made very good friend with three other soldiers. All three of them had been transferred to the 'Kings Own' from 'The Border Regiment'. None had been in trouble like I had (once), but were National Service men just making up the numbers. Each one would only have to serve ten months in this Godforsaken land.

Norman Slater (Norm) was from Fleetwood, a weightlifter, bodybuilder and gymnast.

He was short, but very strong and muscular. A bit of a lad, who knew exactly what he was doing. He became the Company's moneylender and made a small fortune.

Maurice Hubbick (Hubby) was from Carlisle. He was a very good wrestler, and was at one time the Cumberland 'catch-as-catch-can' champion. He also taught me chess; he was a very good tutor, because I could beat him now.

Last, but not least was big Jim Ord (Big Jim), a light-heavyweight boxer of ABA fame. He came from Workington. He stood six feet two inches tall, and was a lean and very hard man, who could also box a little.

All three were to become very good mates indeed. Norm, Hubby and big Jim had about ten months left to serve; I knew that when they went back to the UK I would still have eleven months to go. How the time was dragging; I must keep busy and make the best of things.

The regiment travelled to Seoul by train, simply cattle trucks with windows. As we left Pusan railway station, I saw a man run towards the train and then disappear under the train.

I leapt to the other side of the carriage; I looked through the window and saw this man emerge at the other side of the train. The man's legs had been amputated below the knee; you could see the bones steaming. All of a sudden, two Korean military policemen arrived, and without exchanging a word to the man, shot him twice in the head with a revolver. It was a terrible sight to witness and Norm said to me, "Have you seen a ghost Don?"

I said, "I wish I had, but what I have just witnessed was for real."

Some time later when we were well on our way, the Company Commander (Captain Crossley) explained to us that the man who had been shot and killed was after compensation. He had selected a British Commonwealth train because only the British paid compensation. I thought to myself that the poor chap had selected the wrong train. Such a brutal world we live in.

Chapter 6
Korea

We arrived in Seoul and then transferred to a fleet of three-ton lorries. These lorries would take us to our final destination.

I was in 'Baker' Company (today it would be called 'Bravo').

An infantry regiment comprises six companies: A, B, C, D, HQ (headquarters) and S (Support) companies.

The Commanding Officer is usually a lieutenant colonel.

The Company Commander (CC) is usually a major or a captain. Each company has a warrant officer class II and three platoon sergeants. A company comprises three platoons of infantrymen, each platoon having three sections. Each section led by a junior NCO comprising, eleven men with three or four men in support, these would include signallers and machine gunners.

Korea was a special place. There was no war going on now, but the defences had to be protected, and the best way to do this was to have Lewis, Browning machine guns and Bren guns on tripods firing on fixed lines. Our main line of defence was called 'The Kansas Line'; in the months to come I was going to get to know this fortification, just like I know the back of my hand.

'B' company's campsite was in a shallow valley, just a few hundred metres from the river Imjim. This river, about the same size as the Thames at Oxford, would eventually flow into the river Han that flowed through Seoul, the capital. We were situated south of the town of Panmunjom, where the peace talks were still going on. An armistice was never signed, I doubt if it will ever be signed.

The Royal Engineers had already erected six large marquee type tents. This would house 'B' company. The other companies were a good half a mile from each other, arranged for protection, in case of a surprise attack.

The Company Commander (CC) gave us a brief talk, all about security and the task of getting our camp up to scratch.

The NCO ordered us all to have an early night; we would start in earnest the next day. The entire tent site had to be made level and wooden planking was nailed to joists to give us a better floor. It all took a great deal of time. Having had experience as a joiner, I was put in charge on all the building improvements.

I became very popular with our CC - Captain Crossley - who excused me guard duties whilst working on the camp. I even designed several blocks of wooden loos for the site, all with individual holes and covers.

After six or seven weeks things on the campsite began to look much better.

A new CC (Major Whitworth) took charge of our Company. The major was just out of the French Foreign Legion and was a stickler for discipline. He called us together and read the riot act. He led by example. Taking his cap off, he displayed a shaven head and said, "This is how you will all have your hair; we do not want any little ninnies running wild on your head."

'Christ,' I thought. 'This CC is going to be a tough cookie.'

As the company's joiner, I escorted the CC around the campsite. He did not say a great deal, but he did remark that my toilets were the best he had seen, and suggested that I patent them. Major Whitworth was a real officer, firm yet fair. I was beginning to warm to him and to his very high standards of discipline.

KATCOMs 'Koreans attached to the Commonwealth.' These young men were well educated, and before the conflict had been professional men in commerce, teachers, and several were lawyers and medical students. Their job with us was being interpreters.

Each Company had about a dozen KATCOMs. Those attached to our platoon had the names of Lee Bok Sung and Ho Ming Suk, they were very nice young men and Lee was to become a very good friend.

To avoid conflict these KATCOMs were housed together in their own tent. We were not encouraged to fraternise with them, I do not know the reason, but it appeared to me senior NCOs and officers treated them as second class citizens. I found this form of apartheid very distressing; thankfully over the coming months the KATCOMs were more acceptable and they became a very valuable asset to us all. Lee was at his happiest when he was working with me, and we could discuss all aspects of our different lives. His English improved tremendously, pity I cannot say that about my grasp of Korean.

News came through that a soldier in another company had died from a form of the bubonic plague. Major Whitworth called a meeting and told us that stringent new hygiene procedures would have to come into force.

This illness is transmitted from fleas that infest brown rats. 'Christ! We had enough of them.'

No more eating in the tents, all mess tins to be boiled after use and more bathing to be allowed, albeit in the freezing Imjim.

The CC somehow got hold of a Nissan hut from the Americans; it was to become our new canteen/dining room and recreational venue. Norman was a painter and decorator and he took it upon himself to paint and spruce the place up.

We called our new venue 'The Imjim Inn' and for the next year we would become very fond of our little Inn. Some very good times were in store for many. However, for a very small minority...

Regretfully the KATCOMs were not allowed to use our Inn; again this policy of two classes of people was showing its ugly face yet again. However, we did manage to get a few bottles of beer to them. They were very grateful, but it was for me a very unsatisfactory type of segregation.

The days were fast getting shorter and there was a distinct chill in the air. I had started to take my turn at guard duty. Our main guard duties were carried out on a small hill, just a few yards from the bridge that crossed the river Imjim. The other site that was guarded was the stores and armoury. Major Whitworth insisted that those soldiers who were on guard had to be hidden, out of sight and not wandering about in full view of... I had to agree with his logic. In the meantime, Norman had been promoted to lance corporal (one chevron) which meant he could stay in the bunker whilst we did the observing out in the open.

Smoking was taboo and no naked lights were allowed, however, you could smoke in the bunker, obtaining a light from an ever-smouldering wick. It was after doing several guard duties that I realised it was far easier being a lance corporal (staying in the comfort of the bunker) than facing the elements. I would have to knuckle down and try to gain promotion.

Winter arrived, it was bloody freezing, all training ceased (not guard duties) and it was just an effort to keep dry and warm.

The only time we ventured out was to go to the Imjim Inn for our meals and a pint. Being in a theatre of war we were entitled to a daily rum ration. Many men did not like rum so I made a point of storing the surplus; I soon had a few pints of the stuff.

One cold evening we heard an explosion, the noise had come from the cookhouse. When we arrived at the cookhouse a very sad sight met our view. Our cook, Jock Collins, was covered in flames from head to foot. He was screaming in agony and ran towards the river, but failed to make it. He was very badly burned, poor Jock; he was a diamond of a man and a bloody good cook. Jock was buried with full military honours at the Commonwealth cemetery at Seoul. The cause of this tragedy was a petrol can exploding near to the cook's hot plate. The cookhouse was very badly damaged. Major Whitworth ordered Lee and me to start work on the repairs to the cookhouse.

It was freezing, the wind was blowing in from Siberia and the temperature dropped to minus sixty degrees Fahrenheit.

Lee and I were carrying our repairs to the cookhouse roof; I was standing on an improvised scaffold swinging a sledgehammer at a very large staple. The scaffold collapsed and I fell to the ground, landing on a pile of kitchen utensils. I had only fallen about five feet but I had landed badly. I felt a severe pain in my lower leg and I could not move my neck. Lee and several other lads placed me on a stretcher and set off to take me to the field hospital situated about a quarter of a mile away at HQ. It was the start of a journey I shall never forget, on route to HQ I was accidentally allowed to fall off the stretcher at least three times, each time this occurred I felt severe pain and felt faint. Eventually we arrived at the field hospital.

The medical officer saw me at last and told me that my leg was broken and I had injuries to my upper spine. He placed my neck in a support and placed a splint on the leg. He told me that I would be taken to the main hospital at Seoul, some twenty miles away. Another journey that is best forgotten; fortunately, the medic who travelled with me had a good supply of morphine. Due to the snow and wind, our journey took far longer.

At the hospital, I was x-rayed and the x-ray confirmed that my leg was broken and a disc in my neck was dislocated. My leg was set in plaster and I was fitted with a neck brace.

After a few days, the pain had lessened and I was feeling OK.

One morning an American doctor came to visit me; he informed me that I would be transferred to Japan because the milder climate there would help my leg to heal more quickly.

Next day I was taken to Seoul airport, and I boarded a Dakota type plane and off we went. In a few hours I had my first sight of the snow-capped Mount Fuji.

We landed at an airport not far from Tokyo, from there to the British Commonwealth General Hospital in Kobe. I was to remain here for the next twelve weeks. It was a good hospital and the staff did everything to make you content and comfortable. As usual, I had been writing to my wife and mother on a regular basis, unfortunately they had received none of my letters. In desperation, my mother had seen the local MP and asked him to make inquiries on her behalf.

Some time later the ward sister informed me that the British Consul had made a request to visit me. I thought to myself, 'what the hell does he want?'

A few days later I was in the common room with a Canadian named Fred Lawther. Fred also had his leg in plaster and we had become friends. I saw two high-ranking army officers and another chap enter the room; they came over to me and asked if I was Private Smith.

"Yes", I said.

They introduced themselves as Colonel Bains and Major Calve. The man in civvies was the British Consul.

Major Calve said, "We have come to see how you are getting on Smith; your mother has been very worried, so much so that questions were asked in the House about you. We have apologised to your family for not informing them of your whereabouts and the accident that you had. We also would like to apologise to you.

We will inform your family that you are making good progress and the medical staffs inform us that you will be discharged in the very near future."

Well I was gob smacked. Just like my mother to put the cat amongst the pigeons. I knew now that Jean and my mother would be informed. I wondered if these recent events would get me back home to the UK any sooner.

A week later I was seen by the medical officer and told that I would be discharged in two days' time. I asked where I would be going.

The MO said, "You will be returning to your regiment in Korea."

I was very disappointed, but on reflection, thinking that I would be sent home to the UK was a little optimistic. So a few days later I was issued with the usual bread, cheese and an apple and taken to Tokyo airport where I boarded a Globe master plane. It appeared that I was the only British serviceman on the plane. It was the biggest plane I had ever seen. Two rows of seats around the sides of the plane, upstairs and down, enough seats for 400 troops. I saw three three-ton lorries drive onto the plane, followed by two jeeps.

I thought, 'This plane is never going to get off the ground,' but to my surprise it did get off the ground, but only after plenty of vibrations and deafening noises. We were soon above the clouds; again, Mount Fuji soon came into view.

After about an hour into the flight, female stewardesses came round issuing the US troops with their lunch boxes. What they were being given put my bread and cheese in the shade; I was far too embarrassed to display my food.

A US soldier shouted to a stewardess and said, "For God's sake give this Limey some decent grub."

I was given a plastic box with all kinds of goodies in it.

Three hours later we were over Seoul and the plane had to encircle the airport until a slot was found for us. I looked through the porthole and saw the massive wing of the plane shuddering under the strain. I thought we were never going to land, but land we did, and after disembarking I went to the information officer. He told me that transport would be soon arriving to take me to join my regiment. Two hours later I was back in camp, the sergeant major welcomed me back into the fold and informed me that my departure had caused a few eyebrows to be raised at HQ.

He told me that Major Whitworth had purchased some new timber and wanted me to refurbish the toilets. 'Well!' I thought, 'all this air travel just to mend a shithouse.'

Next day I met up with my mates. Lee was the first to seek me out; he was very pleased to see me. Norman, Jim and Maurice all popped into my tent to say hello. I noticed that all three were wearing a chevron – lance corporals, all three of them. What had I missed?

All were keen to fill me in with the local gossip, many of my mates had departed for the UK and there were many new faces. How a name sticks – everyone now referred to me as 'Smith the Company chippie'. I suppose that I could have been called a lot worse.

The campsite was now looking spick-and-span and spring was in the air. The countryside looked far greener and there was a dense growth of brambles and new shrubs, this made a pleasant change from the landscape that had so recently been devastated by war.

I went for a walk into the countryside and the number of game birds...

I saw pheasants, quail and chukkas; cranes were flying north to the tundra, the sight amazed me. 'I need a gun,' I thought. 'Those birds would make a pleasant change from the company stew.'

Major Whitworth called me into his office and told me that my team was to go to the Kansas Line; to work on the fortifications of our defences.

I thought that it would make a pleasant change from life in the camp. I was right; it made a very pleasant change. I was my own boss and the only orders I received were from the officer (an American) who was in charge of construction. Lee and two other KATCOMs were in my party; we all got on like a house on fire.

I asked the US officer if he could obtain a .22 rifle for me, he said he would do his best. A shotgun would have been better to bag a few birds, but it was hard to obtain the ammunition. These birds were everywhere; after all, they had been undisturbed for over three years.

It was fast becoming summer and the temperature soared a little each day. My gang worked about seven hours a day on the defensive line; it was a series of bunkers and trenches and when finished and fully manned it would be a very secure defence.

Most men would be firing machine guns, fixed on tripods.

When we arrived back at camp there was always a good meal waiting for us, a couple of pints in the Imjim Inn, then off to bed. Because we were out all day on a working party I did not have to do guard duties, in fact I had done very few since arriving in Korea. I hated guard duties because it gave me time to think of home and my wife Jean; I was always thinking of her and my young son.

One day, orders were given for B Company to round up several hundred prisoners who had escaped from Panmunjom. They were heading south to the capital Seoul. We had to act very fast otherwise they would soon be lost if they were allowed to mix with the ordinary people of Seoul. Ammunition was issued to us all, we were warned that the prisoners could also be armed.

We set off in four three-ton lorries; our KATCOMs had to go with us, interpreters would be essential in rounding these escapees up. Lee was speaking to a farm worker; it was obvious to me that the worker had said something of importance to Lee.

Lee went over to the officer and said something to him.

The officer then shouted, "Information received informs us that the escapees are hiding in a cemetery about a mile from here; we will proceed on foot from here."

We were soon at the cemetery (no gravestones - Koreans bury the bones of their dead in large earthenware pots). The escapees had decided to try to conceal themselves behind the pots; not a very good idea, we could see movements behind the pots as soon as we arrived. Lee was ordered to use the loudspeaker and to order the escapees to surrender. We could hear a great deal of talking, then all of a sudden a single escapee appeared from behind a pot and charged at the leading soldiers; he was brandishing a large machete.

Lee shouted out a warning in Korean. The man continued to run toward the troops. All of a sudden, a shot rang out; the man fell to the ground holding his leg. The officer placed his revolver back into his holster. Using the loudspeaker, further instructions were given to the escapees. After more talking amongst themselves all the prisoners came from behind the pots and surrendered.

Lee told me later that the man who charged at us was just making a gesture of defiance; thankfully the officer had aimed for the leg. We arranged for the South Korean military to return the escapees back to Panmunjom. Once there, all prisoners were given the option of returning to the south or to the north of Korea. The choice was theirs, in hindsight I do feel that those opting to go North…

All was going well at the camp; I was very busy with my work on the Kansas Line. Norman and Jimmy were due to return to the UK in a week or so, I would miss them. A week after that and Maurice was to depart as well. Norman had made a really good job of the Imjim Inn; he had painted scenes of the Lancashire countryside on all the walls, it gave the Inn a real homely feeling. I can remember gazing at a painting of Rivington Pike and wishing that I was there, I would have run the six miles to my home but it was only day dreaming. I suffered bouts of homesickness from time to time; after all, I had been away from Jean and my son for well over a year now. The pending departure of my three mates did not help matters.

Just before Norman and Jimmy departed I was called into the CO's office. The CO said to me, "Smith you have done a good job on this camp, you have worked hard. The sergeant major has recommended you for promotion to lance corporal and I endorse his recommendation. Your promotion will take effect from today, well done and congratulations."

The sergeant major patted me on the back and he said to me as I left the office, "I do not think it will be long before you get your second stripe Smith, keep up the good work!"

I felt very pleased with myself and the beer flowed that night.

Soon it was time for Norman and Jimmy to leave, soon after Maurice would be departing. Ah well! The sooner they all get home the sooner it will be my turn. I wrote a long letter to Jeanie, I had written so many times I was beginning to repeat myself. However, I had to keep writing, it was only Jean's letters that kept me sane.

The winter was fast drawing in, it was dark much earlier and there was a distinct nip in the air, especially in the mornings. Cranes, geese and other birds could be seen on their migration south; the parka jacket was to become a very useful garment.

Not much soldiering can be done when the winds blow from Siberia; keep warm and dry was the order of the day.

Winter arrived, Christ it was cold. All we could do was to keep warm and do a few exercises every day. Our main duties were weapon cleaning and guard duty. One night I was in charge of the guard, guarding the bridge. To ensure that we were not unduly disturbed, and to give us prior notice of an intruder, I arranged for some green twine to be placed about fifty yards around our command post. Tin cans, filled with pebbles, were secured to the twine at irregular intervals.

We could smoke in the command post but the sentries on stand-to could not. Being the NCO, I was warm and snug in my parka and sleeping bag; all I had to do was to ensure that the sentries were changed over on time. I did a little reading and would write letters to my wife and parents.

One night the cans rattled, it could be an animal or a bird that had caused the noise. Not taking any chances, I ordered the guard to standby, and to be ready for whatever action was necessary. I went outside the command post and secreted myself behind a snow-covered bush. I could see the silhouettes of two men approaching, I whispered for every one to be silent. When the figures were within range of my Sten gun, I shouted, "Halt! Who goes there, friend or foe?"

One of the visitors shouted, "Friend, it is the CO and duty sergeant major."

I replied, "What is the password?"

The reply was, "George Formby."

I replied, "Pass friends, hands on your head and come and identify yourselves."

"Corporal Smith, I am the duty sergeant major and this gentleman is your CO. We are impressed by your alertness; now turn out the guard for inspection."

The CO inspected the guard and joked that he could not stay for a cup of tea. The CO said it was far too cold to stay out by the river, which at the time was frozen solid.

As they left the CO said, "Whose idea was it to stake out the tin cans?"

"It was mine," I said.

The CO replied, "Not in army regulations Smith, but a damn good idea."

This Arctic weather made it impossible to do anything other than guard duties, weapon training and PE; a few tots of rum and a good kip helped to pass the time, however, it did not pass quickly enough for me.

Apart from my time spent in Japan, I had now been in Korea for nearly fourteen months, I was fast becoming the old man of the regiment. In April, I would be celebrating my 21st birthday on bloody guard on the bridge over the river; my mother had requested the Commonwealth Forces Radio to play her favourite tune, *Green Sleeves*, on my big date. I listened to the request, not my type of music, but it was the thought; my mates did a little leg-pulling.

My birthday passed and spring was now with us. The countryside was in bloom, the birds were returning from their winter migration. My time in Korea was ending, just a few months to go. Jean how I miss you! At last, I could see light at the end of the tunnel. I was informed that I would be a member of the advance party to Hong Kong.

Just before I left Korea, I was promoted to full corporal.

It was good to be sailing south to Hong Kong; I was on my way home, albeit just one more place to pass the seven months I had to serve, Christ! I was homesick. Best foot forward and again make the best of a bad job.

Summer was around the corner; it was getting very warm.

When we arrived in the port of Kowloon, we were all transported to the village of Lock Ma Chou in the New Territories, about thirty miles inland and only a mile or so from the Chinese border.

I had been transferred to Charlie Company and I found out that I was in charge of a platoon (three sections – about thirty soldiers). It was to turn out the best time of my service. OK! Unlike Korea there were bullshit parades and anti-malaria tablet parades every morning. That was my main function of the day, making sure everyone swallowed their anti-malaria tablet.

To miss taking the medicine was a very serious offence.

My day consisted of participating in sport, boxing, soccer and competitive swimming. I was very lucky and represented my regiment at many sports. What a life! Nevertheless, how I miss my Jean.

The summer came and it was soon approaching my discharge date, time was dragging and I was suffering from acute gate fever. I put everything into my sport and I was as fit as a fiddle. I was still boxing at middleweight, but I had a weight gain problem. I had to train really hard to maintain my boxing weight. I was advised to eat less, this was difficult so opted to reduce my recreational fluid intake, and this appeared to do the trick.

I was selected to represent the Hong Kong brigade at a boxing contest in Malaya about a thousand miles south from Hong Kong. We went by ship, as aeroplanes were not at the disposal of other ranks in those days. A week's cruise in the South China Sea, what a life! Good food and training every day made our team nearly unbeatable, well almost, only time would tell.

We arrived in Singapore and were transported to a beautiful little village named Tanglin. The facilities were great, a full-size gym and a lovely pool set in beautiful tropical gardens.

The boxing was much more than I had anticipated. The Americans had imported all their Golden Glove champions to take part. With the Yanks it was not just about sport, but prestige. They had to win everything, whatever the cost. They had in fact sent their Olympic boxing team. Well I was the only one to win against the USA, the referee stopping the fight in my favour because my opponent sustained a very bad cut due to a clash of heads. I enjoyed my stay in Malaya, how I wish Jean could have been there with me. After two weeks of luxury living, I returned to Hong Kong.

I was now enjoying being an acting sergeant, my duties were varied and very rewarding, this combined with my sporting activities made the time go fast.

On 4 July 1955, I at last set sail for the UK. I was so excited; I was now counting the hours, even the minutes.

The ship was forced to return home via the Panama Canal because of troubles in the Suez Canal area.

We sailed to Vancouver then south to Panama, through the canal then up to Boston and across the Atlantic to Liverpool.

The routine on the passage home was very relaxed, because ninety per cent of the troops were on their way home to be discharged and back into civvies.

It was five o'clock when the officer on watch announced over the Tannoy system that we had arrived in Liverpool. I rushed on deck and behold, there was the Liver building right in front of me.

Home at last after two years, nine months away from my wife and family. Things will certainly get better from now on. Jeanie! I am on my way.

Chapter 7
HM Prison Strangeways

B ack home at last. In 1960 I was invited for an
interview at HM Prison Strangeways, Manchester.
What a gloomy place I thought, as I approached those
forbidding prison gates. I handed my letter of
introduction to the officer who opened the gate.

"Come in; take your hands out of your pockets, and
everyone in here is called Sir! Except the bloody convicts,
got it?"

I thought, 'I am back in the bloody army!'

Later I had a medical check and had to do an IQ test.

I was told that I had passed so far, and that a governor
grade and the Principal Training Officer would interview
me. I will never forget this interview. The governor
grade, by the name of Mr Brown, had a very badly
disfigured face, scarred and burned. Therefore, whoever
asked the questions I always looked at the Principal
Officer when giving my answers.

After several minutes Mr Brown said in a very
commanding voice, "Young man, you can look at me, my
face will not bite you. It was caused during the war."

These remarks by Mr Brown gave me much more
confidence. I did look at his face and beneath that face
was a very brave man. Both interviewers were ex-
servicemen; so most of the interview was about Korea
and my service in the army. A subject I was well familiar
with. At the conclusion of the interview, Mr Brown

informed me that they both agreed I would be suitable for training as a prison officer.

As I left the room Mr Brown said, "Thank you for looking at me when talking to me. It makes a great difference for everyone, but especially for me."

I could not wait to get home to inform Jean of my success. The future looked very rosy.

Since that time, I have never had any difficulty looking anyone in the face. Mr Brown, who was the Deputy Governor, was a very brave man. He was later to become one of the most senior directors in the whole of HM Prison Service. He also became responsible for many prison reforms.

Two other new recruits were under training with me.

For the next four weeks we were under the care of the prison training officer, a nice man who was very dedicated to his work. We wore civilian clothes and had the HMP badge pinned to our lapel. All the prisoners referred to us as 'fishy'. I could not see the connection until I realised that POUT was the acronym for 'Prison Officer under Training'. Pout is also an abbreviation for pouting, which is a salt-water fish. So, at last I was learning something.

We were attached to an officer and visited all the various departments, making notes on what we had observed in each department. Every officer in charge of us would stress the importance of locating where the alarm bell was situated in each building. How important this advice was to prove during the rest of my service. I had always been very fit, so the physical training side of the course came very easy.

Basic assessment training had now been completed; we were given several days leave and ordered to report back to Strangeways the following Monday.

Ken, Phil, and I were sitting in the staff room awaiting our final instructions. There were always about twenty spare officers on standby, just in case an alarm bell went off.

The alarm bell was quite a common sound at Strangeways, usually just a fight between two prisoners, at odds with each other.

When an alarm bell rang all officers ran at speed to the location of the trouble. The Centre Principal Officer, who would have seen the 'location tag' drop when the bell was pressed, would call out the location of the trouble to all staff, as they passed by the Control Centre.

In the staff room, they would be playing cards or reading their newspapers.

On one occasion the alarm bell sounded. Everyone with the exception of Ken, Phil and I, leapt to their feet and departed at great speed. We just carried on talking. The Chief Officer came into the staff room.

"What the hell are you three pricks doing sat on your arses? That was an alarm bell and in my prison everyone answers a bell."

"Well sir, we have no keys and no uniform," I said nervously.

The Chief Officer said, "Bollocks, no excuse. You follow the rest of the staff and observe what is going on when you get there. Now off you go, and observe the incident. I want you to write what you observe in your training note books; let me have sight of your observations at the end of the week."

We arrived at the scene of the trouble. There was a prisoner on the roof of a workshop. He was shouting obscenities and telling everyone that he was an innocent man. Two works officers had already erected a long ladder and were about to go onto the roof to remove him. The Chief Officer had arrived on the scene and bawled, "On his own accord he can use the ladder, I'm not risking the lives of my staff for that stupid cunt."

The prisoner continued to shout all the obscenities that he knew. The Chief shouted, "You have three minutes to agree to come down, or I will put the hose pipes on you and flush you off."

"Piss off," the prisoner shouted back.

I was flabbergasted; I had never witnessed anything like this before.

Works staff started to unravel the power hoses. When all the power hoses were ready, the Chief shouted to the prisoner,

"Are you coming down?"

"Piss off," the prisoner replied.

"OK!" the Chief Officer said. "Let the water flow; just put it on half pressure to start with."

You could see the pressure building up inside the hose pipes. The Chief said to the works officer operating the hose, "Just give him a wetting; he might just think I am not bluffing."

A single hose was turned on. The prisoner was drenched to the skin in seconds. The prisoner shouted,

"OK! I will come down." He came down the ladder and was removed to the segregation unit.

As the Chief Officer left the scene he came over to us and said, "Forget those notes I ordered you to make. I do not want this incident recording, understand?"

All three of us got the message. An effective method, but rather cruel, I thought. However, no prisoner ever went onto the roof of a prison building at Strangeways for over twenty years.

Monday arrived and I noticed that there were now only two of us. Phil the ex-sailor had failed the assessment.

I was very surprised because of the three of us I thought he was the best suited. I asked the training officer why he had not made it, and he said, "None of your business, but had you not passed I do not think he would have had the bottle to ask me why you had failed. Dig the gist?"

We were then taken to the 'Number One Governor' who congratulated us, and informed us that we would be sent to HM Prison Training College at Leyhill in Gloucestershire. We were given rail warrants and two days leave, then off we went for a well-earned weekend with our families.

Chapter 8
Leyhill Prison

Ken and I arrived at Leyhill in the late afternoon. We were instructed to attend a meeting at seven o'clock to meet the Principal of the college, a Commander Hawkins. The 'Boss', as we later called him amongst ourselves, was a big man who reminded me of Jack Hawkins, the actor – could have been his brother. He was a very smart man, who spoke with a posh Oxford accent.

"Welcome to Leyhill. So you all want to become prison officers; my job is to prove that you are good enough to wear the Queen's uniform. I shall make it as hard as I can for you. Good luck!" he said.

I thought to myself that this is going to be bloody worse than the army. However, I took a liking to the 'Boss' from day one; he was a man's man. What made Leyhill so nice was the accommodation. It had at one time been a large stately mansion, beautiful rooms, velvet curtains, a spiral staircase, lovely gardens with many varieties of trees, and the food was top class. There were forty students, ten in each of four sections, all in alphabetical order, with their own Principal Training Officer. The training was so devised that the sections competed against each other at everything, especially on the parade ground, in the gym and at the lectures. I had no problems in the gym, or marching for two hourly sessions a day. I had been a drill instructor in the army so it was a 'piece of cake'. Being an ex-drill instructor, I soon shaped my section into looking like the Guards on parade. The technical stuff I had to work at very hard, mostly at night, as well as into the early hours of the morning on some occasions.

The training at the college was hard but I enjoyed the challenge. I did have to put extra time and effort into the writing of the essays and the technicalities of prison rules. There are many facts and data to remember. With will-power and the loss of much sleep, I kept pace with the other students.

In the second week of our training, we were introduced to judo. The expert was a Mr Long. He had more black belts than the whole of the Thames Valley police force well; he gave us that impression. I was in section four, which contained the men with the last letters of the alphabet. Therefore, it was Richards to Smith D (me), then to number ten - Billy Wright. At number seven was a great big Scot by the name of Smollett. He was built like a brick shithouse, all seventeen stones of him. Being the next in size, I was paired with this highland gorilla.

I dreaded the judo session; I was thrown from pillar to post, wall to wall, from one mat to another. Had I requested a change of partner I would have been called 'chicken'. After about a dozen or so sessions, the big Scot threw me over to the wall and I broke one of my toes. That was a godsend; however, I thought that they would not allow me to finish the course. I did not want to start all over again. I saw the 'Boss' who decided that I had made enough progress and I could now sit out all physical exercises, drill, and judo sessions.

On the last day of the judo sessions Mr Long, the self-proclaimed 'judo king', made a challenge to anyone in the section to tackle him.

"Come on, I can only kill you," he snarled.

Big Jock Smollett ran on to the mats, picked Mr Long up like a sack of spuds and threw him to the ground.

Mr Long cried, "That's not bloody judo!"

Smollett said, "No! But very effective."

Old Mr Long did not know where to look. He had been caught off guard. Big Jock and I became good friends.

Training over, it was now time to find out who had passed and who had failed. A few days earlier we had been asked to state our preference of the type of establishment we wanted to be posted to. With my interest in sports and my military background, I opted for a detention centre. 'Anywhere in the UK will suit me fine,' I thought.

I considered it would be much more interesting working with youngsters, rather than old lags; the disciplined routine at a detention centre appealed to me.

There were two rooms. If you were called into the room on the left you had failed the course; issued with a rail warrant and your cash that was due was paid. Those that had failed were then taken to another part of the college, and were never seen again by those who had passed.

Of the forty that had started the training, several had been sent packing before the end of training; mainly for misbehaviour, or being unsuitable for reasons known only to the staff. Only 26 were successful. I was one who was fortunate enough to pass; better still, I obtained the posting of my choice. This was a junior detention centre at Buckley Hall in Rochdale, Lancashire. The centre was just twelve miles from my home town of Bolton.

Looking back, this was the turning point in the lives of all my family. Our fifth child, Barbara, had just been born. This was the fresh start I had needed; I do feel that the training I had received to become a prison officer had made me a better person. Although Jeanie, my wife, might not agree. Back to Manchester for my uniform, Buckley Hall here I come!

Chapter 9
HM Detention Centre
Buckley Hall

I left Leyhill Training College feeling very happy and content with myself. I arrived home late at night. Jean, my wife, had allowed all the children to stay up late to greet me. We had a lot of hugs and kisses and everyone was excited about our future move. Although we were only going to Rochdale, some twenty miles away, it did feel like we were all going to Australia.

Next day I had to go to Strangeways prison at Manchester to collect my uniform. On arrival I was met by an officer, taken to the prison stores and given two very large boxes.

I asked the storeman, "Do I need to see if all the uniform fits?" The storeman replied, "It will fit you, I measured you up and I've been doing it for nearly 30 years."

Some time later I caught the train back to Bolton. The children had arrived home from school; their first demand was, 'Try your new uniform on dad!'

First thing to do was to fit the insignia and fix the cap badge. We were issued with two of everything. The only items of clothing not issued were the black socks; I would have to buy some. I had been given a week's leave before joining the staff at the detention centre.

With my boots shining and sharp creases in my trousers, I was feeling ten feet tall. It was just like it had always been when I was in the army. I was proud to be back in uniform again, it always gave me a feeling of confidence. I got the train from Bolton to Rochdale, and then I took a taxi to Buckley Hall, which was situated on the other side of town.

When I arrived at Buckley Hall I alighted from the taxi and as I stood outside this very large old mansion, I wondered just what the future might hold. I knocked on the big heavy door; it was the largest doorknocker in the world, what a noise it made. A short, stocky prison officer opened the door. I handed him my documents of introduction; he seemed to take hours reading them. He then said, "So you are Officer Smith? I am Officer Barry, welcome to the SSSS."

I did not question his abbreviation. Later I found it to mean Short, Sharp, Shock, Shithouse. I offered to shake hands, he declined. I would never make that offer again to this officer.

As we passed by the gate lodge (key safe room) there were six or seven trainees in a line waiting to see the Warden (Governor). Officer Barry moved down the line and smacked everyone of them across the face. Obviously done to impress me, it didn't; it had the opposite effect.

I thought he was an arsehole and some weeks later I told him so. I soon found out that Officer Barry was the only sadist, bully and braggart employed at Buckley Hall.

It had been my misfortune to meet Officer Barry on my first day. I was to have many meetings and confrontations with Officer Barry over the next few years. Staff and inmates referred to Officer Barry as 'Adolf'; very appropriate I thought.

I was introduced to the Warden and Deputy Warden (Chief Officer); both shook my hand as if they meant it, this made me feel very welcome.

They explained to me the basics of the routine and what was expected of me. We discussed my service in the army, the Deputy Warden saying that they needed an experienced drill instructor.

They said they would see me the following day after I had met the Administration Officer to arrange my temporary living accommodation and I was told to go and have a bite to eat and fix up my accommodation with the Administration Officer. I would also need to sort out my pay and expenses that were due to me.

I would reside in the bachelor quarters until a quarter became available for my family. It would be about eighteen months before my family joined me as there was an acute shortage of officer's family accommodation.

We all worked late and early shifts. This meant that I could volunteer to sleep in the centre every other night and go home every other day at 1.30 p.m. Therefore, this allowed me to spend twenty hours or so with my wife and children.

I purchased a 'Honda 90' motor cycle, which now meant I was only thirty or so minutes away from home. It was obvious now that staff and trainees referred to me as 'Honda Smith'. I suppose they could have given me a worse nickname.

I was seconded to an Officer Roberts for a month. He was an excellent officer, also a nice person. Well over six feet tall and very smart. A Welshman with a little turned up nose. He had been in the service for about ten years. He knew it all; a very quiet man, with not a great deal to say, but what he did say always appeared to make sense.

Taffy Roberts became my role model; time proved that I had made the right choice.

The daily routine for staff and trainees was very harsh. The trainees were out of their dormitory beds at six o'clock. Then out on the yard for twenty-five minutes of non-stop PE. Back to their dormitories, for a wash, shave, and make-up their bed packs. Breakfast was at a quarter to eight, and then it was off to the workshops until twelve noon. Lunch was at quarter past twelve. Then it was back to the workshops until quarter to five. Throughout the day each workshop would be allocated circuit training and drill for one hour every day.

It was a very vigorous routine both for staff and trainees. As you would expect, I soon became the first choice drill instructor. I did enjoy playing the sergeant major, however, I would suspect that the trainees had other ideas about my 'about-turns', 'left-right-left-rights', et-ceteras.

Weekends were more relaxed, both for staff and inmates. We had two soccer pitches and a volley ball court. All inmates were encouraged to participate in the weekend activities. Sunday morning, we all went to church, according to our religious denominations. You could not be an atheist in a detention centre, which I thought wrong. A religion is a personal choice. Well, more often than not, religion is installed in the brain by your parents or other well-meaning people.

Sunday morning was cleaning day. This was followed by the Warden's inspection. All kit and clothing was inspected, along with teeth, hands and in some cases, toenails.

The Warden never missed a trick. A dusty locker could cost a trainee three days' remission or loss of privileges, or both. These inspections were necessary for several reasons: they ensured that the inmates were clean and that the clothing and bedding et cetera was serviceable. It was just like being in the army all over again, and I loved every minute of it.

Every trainee had free and open access to speak with the Warden or Visiting Magistrate by just making a formal request.

All the trainees were clean and very well fed; because of the vigorous routines they had to adhere to, they needed extra food. When they first arrived at the establishment most of them were cocky and awkward; given time, they became much more respectful and settled into the routine. It was harder for some, away from mother for the very first time, some were homesick. There were tears; for the majority it was their first time away from home, even a so-called hard case can miss his parents.

An officer at a detention centre needed to understand, he had to care; most did. You had to look out for the bullies; you seem to get these in all occupations. Overall, we coped very well at Buckley Hall.

It was a prison rule that on reception the Medical Officer, the Welfare Officer and the Warden would see every new trainee within the first 24 hours of his reception. This procedure had to be strictly adhered to.

I well remember when taking over from the evening staff to start a night shift and I was informed that we had received a new reception. The officer told me that he had been fed and appeared to be OK. Receptions are always located in a cubicle (locked), until seen by the reception office. In most cases the trainees would be seen the following morning and then located on a dormitory along with the other trainees.

On this occasion a lad had been received from a Crown Court and had been received very late in the evening, he would be seen the following morning. A Crown Court Judge could sentence a young offender to a detention sentence order without first notifying the Warden to confirm if the centre had a vacancy. Magistrate's Courts on the other hand, had to ensure that the centre had a vacancy. These receptions were usually received between five-o'clock and eight. This allowed all reception procedures to take place. It would also ensure that all the new arrivals were located in a dormitory. In all cases a medical officer at any court should always have examined the trainees, to ensure that they were fit enough to do the sentence at a detention centre.

I checked the number of inmates in the dormitories; we usually had about a hundred trainees in custody at any one time. The day staff handed over all responsibilities to me. Then the main staff went off duty. I went to check on the late arrival. I looked through the cubicle spy-hole and, to my horror, I saw an artificial leg propped up against the wall.

I thought, 'Someone is in serious trouble'. Young men sentenced to a term of detention must be 100 percent fit. I peered into the cubicle again to ensure I was not seeing things that were not true. Sure enough, the young lad who had arrived late only had one leg. I knew he could not be legally held in a detention centre; I had to do something, and fast.

I had to inform the Warden at once; I telephoned his home. His housekeeper informed me he was making an after-dinner speech at the Town Hall, a guest of Cyril Smith MP.

I telephoned the police and requested that I needed to contact the Warden as soon as possible. About ten minutes later the Warden telephoned me and said, "It had better be bloody important, Officer Smith."

When told of the one-legged inmate he said, "Is this a bloody joke or are you pissed?"

I replied, "It is not a joke sir; I never drink when on duty."

The Warden arrived at the centre within minutes.

The night security routine had to be activated to allow the Warden into the centre. As I opened the door the Warden said, "It looks like there has been a right cock-up."

The Warden knocked on the cubicle door, so as not to alarm our new arrival. I opened the door and the Warden and I entered. Looking at the false leg the Warden said, "I just do not believe it."

(The Warden never would swear or curse in the presence of trainees).

"Well, young man, you cannot stay here. Have you been seen by a doctor?"

The lad replied, "No sir."

The Warden said, "I know just what has to be done and quickly. Officer Smith, get a night patrol officer to telephone the Medical Officer and inform him to get over here as soon as possible. Open up reception and prepare to discharge this lad." The young trainee was gob-smacked.

The Warden required the Medical Officer to witness what had been a very serious mistake and a grave injustice. The trainee was dressed in his civilian clothes, given a discharge grant from the Warden's own pocket. The Warden asked the lad if he had somewhere to go at this late hour.

"Yes sir, my mother will be at home in Oldham."

The Warden then arranged for a taxi to take the lad home, and said, "You will take the lad home Officer Smith, with a police escort, and ensure that you explain to his mother that I will sort things out with the trial Judge first thing in the morning. In the meantime, I will take over your duties until you return."

The lad's mother was very pleased to see her son.

She said to him, "Did you not tell them at court you only had one leg?"

The lad said, "I didn't think it mattered."

(Just for the record, the only custodial sentence the Judge could have made was imprisonment; had the Judge been aware of the lad's medical condition I doubt very much if a custodial sentence would have been ordered.)

As I left the lad's home I told him to try to keep out of trouble from now on. His mother thanked me and I returned to the centre.

On my return to the centre the Warden said to me, "All correct Mr Smith. Have a full report on my desk first thing in the morning; someone is in the shit."

The Warden then left the centre and went home. I secured the establishment again. Next morning the orderly room roll board was showing one hundred and two. One too many! The Warden had forgotten to take the one-legged lad off the total roll. I did not have the bottle to tell him when next I saw him. However, I did tell him some weeks later when we were at a social event; he took it in good faith.

As I have written previously, the Warden, Mr Carmichael, was a gentleman.

Time seemed to fly. I was enjoying my work, although it did involve working a great deal of overtime. I had never been so well off financially. My family had now joined me and all the children of school age had soon settled into their new environments, these were very happy days.

I spent a week's detached duty at Risley Remand Centre, mainly staffing the Crown Courts. I found myself working with Officer Barry, mainly supervising prisoners on remand, awaiting trial. He was not the hard man he wanted to appear with the trainees back at Buckley Hall when he was dealing with grown-up men. It was whilst on this tour of detached duty that I confronted him about his bullying. I told him that if I ever saw him hit a trainee again I would report him to the Warden, or alternatively he could have a go at me in the gym. He made no comment, because he knew I was serious.

A few months later I was in the 'Boot Room' (a room where the trainees changed their gym shoes for their boots, ready to go to the workshops).

A trainee came from inside the shower area and his nose was bleeding.

I asked the lad what had happened.

He said, "I fell in the showers sir."

I then noticed Officer Barry leaving the shower room; he was rubbing his knuckles and grinning. I then sent the lad to see the Medical Officer.

Later that evening I went to see the lad who had earlier had his nose injured. I asked him had Officer Barry caused the injury.

The lad, said, "Yes!"

I advised the lad to make a complaint, but he said, "What's the use in here that shit gets away with murder."

I told the lad not to swear and again advised him to make an official complaint.

The lad said, "What's the use?"

Next day Officer Barry and I were alone in the staff room. I confronted him about the lad with the blooded nose.

Officer Barry said, "So what! I did hit the little twat; anyway he had given me a dirty look!"

I told Officer Barry that if the lad made a complaint I would tell the truth about what I saw in the changing room and what the lad had said to me.

Officer Barry said, "That would make you very popular with the staff, I must say!"

I understood what he meant; loyalty amongst staff was very important, but there was a limit to how much I could stand. I told Officer Barry that I had given him a warning about his brutality when we were at the Crown Court. The time had arrived for me to take action. It was time to stand up and be counted.

I said to Officer Barry, "I am going to report you to the Deputy Warden, if that makes me unpopular, so be it."

Officer Barry said, "You haven't got the bottle."

I told the Branch Secretary of our Union of my intention. He said, "If you need to do it, you must do it; I have always said give a horse enough rope… I do agree with you, he has had it coming for years."

I did report the incident to the Deputy Warden, who interviewed the aggrieved trainee. Officer Barry appeared before the Warden, received a severe reprimand and was transferred to another establishment, post-haste. I found to my surprise that my status among my fellow officers had been raised; I had obviously done the right thing.

After his discharge the trainee in question sued the Prison Department for damages and was successful.

Buckley Hall was a far better place now; I was now the official drill instructor. The demise of Officer Barry reminded me of an incident on the yard. Every now and then you would get a trainee who, no matter how much he tried, could not march. What we called, in the army, two left feet. It was pointless allowing this type of lad to be humiliated. I would send them back to the gym or to a workshop. Officer Barry loved to humiliate these lads.

He would get them to march round the perimeter of the yard on their own. He thought it a big laugh and a joke.

One day as I watched Officer Barry walking to his car I noticed that he had the same fault. His left arm went forward with the left leg, now that is what I call justice.

There is nothing worse than having a bully amongst your staff. Some officers tend to be attracted to the bully, although not being bullies themselves. Other members of staff just turn a blind eye. I can say in all honesty that I had only met one bully up to now. I now know just how to deal with them in the future. There is no place in prisons for bullies, be they staff or prisoners.

It was not all doom and gloom at the Detention Centre. We did have some happy times. The trainees on the whole gained great benefit from the training; most certainly you could see the difference when they were discharged.

Buckley Hall was a short-term Junior Detention Centre. We received young men aged from seventeen to twenty, mostly sent to us for a maximum of three months. Those sentenced to six months and over were transferred to HM Detention Centre at Swinfen Hall, in Staffordshire. Emphasis on physical fitness was the main source of the training, education coming a close second.

It is alarming to find how many youths we received could not even read or write. These inmates would receive extra tuition and it is surprising what they could learn in an eight to twelve-week period. Our education tutors worked very hard to achieve the high standards they reached. Many started to study for 'O' levels.

Sport and physical training played another major role. Our instructors were all ex-navy or ex-army physical training instructors. Old Pop Phillips had been a gymnast in the Commonwealth games; it was good to watch him on the parallel bars, at one time he had been the British champion. There was soccer ever Saturday and Sunday and the standard of play was very high. Staff and inmates competed against each other and there was seldom any foul play or ill feelings.

Attached to the establishment were three large rooms which had been converted into a hospital wing. In charge of the hospital was a fully-trained hospital officer who was a fully qualified state registered nurse (SRN)

Every day the duty doctor would telephone in to see if any of the trainees needed his services.

We got a few broken bones on the sports fields and a few black eyes, but seldom anything of a serious nature that needed transferring to the local hospital.

In any penal establishment, the golden rules are preservation of life and the security of our charges. Like a great many public services, staff have to cover the evenings and the night period. The night period we referred to as 'lock-up time'. During this period, all the trainees are locked-up in their respective dormitories and are checked at irregular intervals by the night patrol officers. These men are usually retired prison officers or other retired service personnel.

We had hardly any trouble from the trainees during the night. Although one incident stands out, I was 'sleeping-in' as night orderly officer, when my telephone rang. I answered the telephone. The night patrol officer informed me that he had heard the sound of breaking glass, coming from the direction of the hospital wing.

I dressed, unlocked my room and went with the NP officer to investigate. On opening the door I could see that a bed was unoccupied and that the wire mesh that covered the window had been removed and the glass window broken. I peered towards the ground outside and there in a heap was a trainee by the name of Cooper. I knew straight away that he was badly injured, because he had been admitted to hospital earlier in the day with a broken leg, which he had sustained whilst playing soccer. The ironic thing about this (attempted escape?) is that he was due to complete his sentence in two weeks' time. I telephoned for an ambulance and unlocked the centre.

I walked over to Cooper and said to him, "Why? You had only a couple of weeks to go, now you have broken the cast, and most likely caused more damage to your leg, you stupid sod. What are you?"

He replied, "I am a stupid sod sir."

The lad was in great pain. There was nothing I could do and I just had to await the arrival of the ambulance. I could hear the ambulance in the distance and a police car had responded as well.

The lad, who was in great pain said, "Sorry Mr Smith but I wanted my mother."

I told the ambulance men to take him to hospital. He did not need an escort, with a broken leg and only a couple of weeks left to do he was not a security risk, and the only place he was going was to the hospital. I secured the centre and wrote out my report of the incident for the Warden's attention. Cooper came back to the Centre early the same morning with his plaster cast repaired, and as he passed me, his face went as red as a beetroot.

Cooper said, "I was a silly sod Mr Smith".

We were always very short of staff and great demands were made on all of us to cover the duties of running the centre. Overtime, whilst not compulsory, was done on a voluntary basis to help everyone out, and it was not uncommon to work double shifts; in excess of one hundred hours a week could be worked. Having a day off was like a holiday. The take home pay was very good, but you missed out with the upbringing of your children. We had five children now, David - twelve, Donald - eight, Donna - seven, Susan - five and Barbara - two. Just how Jeanie coped, I will never know; I think the children thought they did not have a father, seldom was I at home.

The wood-chopping shop was one of our most profitable industries. We purchased old railway sleepers and made firewood, to be sold on to a wholesaler. It was good work for the trainees; everyone wanted to use the double-handed cross-cut saws, rather than to chop the sticks. On one occasion, I was on duty with a younger officer in the wood-chopping workshop. All of a sudden, without any prior warning, a fight broke out between several white lads and some black lads, which was a rare event at Buckley Hall. Normally, everyone seemed to get on well together. I saw one lad pick up an axe (the ideal object to keep in a penal establishment) and start to swing it at a group of black lads. I pressed the alarm bell, then ran over to the lad with the axe and shouted, "Give that axe to me, now."

It was obvious that the lad with the axe was as frightened as we all were. He shyly handed me the axe. By this time staff had responded to the alarm bell and rushed into the workshop. Not being able to recognise all those involved, I ordered that all the trainees be returned to the main establishment. Later I identified four of the fighters and charged them all with causing an affray. Because the lad with the axe had handed it over at once he was also charged with the same lesser offence. When the Governor read my reports he decided that the firewood shop was not worth the risk. Many others, including me, agreed. The firewood shop became the 'toy shop' where the trainees would paint small plastic cowboys and Indians (without axes).

The centre's kitchen was the hub of the establishment with a fully-trained prison officer 'cook and baker'. All the trainees' food was prepared by him, and six or seven trainees who had shown an interest in catering ran the kitchen. The cook and baker's name was Taffy Jones, a man of few words, but a man who knew his trade and would not tolerate any nonsense. All the trainees received extra rations than normal prisoners would, because their routine was very demanding and they needed those extra calories to survive the rigorous routines. The food they received was wholesome and nourishing and there were always extras to be had. Mealtimes were sombre, no talking and at six o'clock when they had finished their meal, all the trainees would fold their arms and listen to the six o'clock news.

I well remember one incident when things did not follow the normal pattern. Two trainees started to fight, both using the metal meal trays as weapons. Six officers were on duty in the dining room, three at either end. By previous arrangement, all the trainees stood up and blocked our way to the fight. We had an organised riot on our hands. No trainee actually struck any staff; their task was to just bar our way from getting to the scene of the fight. The alarm bell had been rung and other staff arrived including the Deputy Warden. Prison officers do not carry truncheons in a detention centre, however, long staves are kept securely locked in the Governor's office in case of a riot or other serious disorder. The Deputy Warden, seeing that the situation was getting out of hand, shouted at the top of his voice, "Issue staves."

A still silence followed and all the prisoners returned to their tables and sat on their chairs.

The two fighters – fighting to see who was 'boss man' - were bleeding profusely and were bundled off to the centre's hospital wing. The Deputy Warden read the riot act and he told all the hundred or so trainees that there would be no evening educational classes or association or games in the gym that evening.

The Deputy Warden then said to the staff, "I want all of these scumbags locking in their dormitories, and they will all be charged with causing an affray. The two fighters will have the book thrown at them, including causing a riot. Clear the dining room at once."

You could hear a pin drop as they all stood up and went to their rooms, row after row.

That evening all the staff stayed on duty, just as a precaution, and to start the mammoth task of making out all the charge sheets, even the civilian clerk was called in from her home to assist.

By this time the number one Warden had arrived. He just said, "Are we getting too soft or what? An example will be made."

Every trainee had been charged with the lesser charge of causing a disturbance. Had they been charged with causing a riot or an affray the cases would have had to go before the visiting magistrates or even to an outside court.

Next day 101 trainees assembled in the dining room. Staff had turned out to full capacity; even the cook and the trades officers were dressed in their uniforms. There was an officer about every ten yards around the dining room and in the centre of the dining room had been placed a table and three chairs. The Warden, Deputy Warden and the clerk entered the room. The Warden read out the charge, "That on the date, time, and place stated you all caused a disturbance in the dining room."

The senior officer who had been witness to the incident gave out the evidence. The Warden then said, "You have all heard the evidence, how do you plead? If you are not guilty, stand up."

Only six trainees did stand up. The Warden then said, "Very well, I shall give those standing the benefit of the doubt and I find you not guilty. Now, get them out of here Officer Brown. The rest I find you all guilty and you will all lose fourteen days' remission – no association, no recreational activities for 28 days. Education classes will not be affected; neither will those working in essential jobs be affected during the working day. Clear them all off to their rooms, staff."

Not one trainee uttered a sound. The visiting magistrates dealt with the two fighters and they were transferred to Swinfen Hall Detention Centre in Staffordshire.

I was the officer detailed to cover the entry to the centre, near to the front, on one particular News Year's Eve. It was my bad luck to be on night duty at the door. When the senior officer had locked the entire exterior doors and gates of the centre, he isolated me from the rest of the centre by locking the main door to the dormitories. The senior officer (orderly-officer) would proceed to his room inside the centre. Both of us would go to our individual sleep-in rooms and lock ourselves in. In case of an emergency, the night patrol officers would rouse the senior officer who in turn would inform me of what action to take.

Only the sleep-in officers had access to the keys that could unlock the entire centre. At about 05.30 hrs, the senior sleep-in officer would telephone the sleep-in officer at the gate and proceed to unlock all doors and gates in readiness for the arrival of the day staff.

The trainees were woken at six o'clock by a bell, which was rung by one of the three night patrol officers who had been on live duty all night. The day staff would arrive on duty at six o'clock. A roll check of the trainees would be taken, and the senior night duty officer (orderly-officer) would hand over the control of the centre to the senior officer of the day staff. All trainees would wear gymnasium clothing, and their hectic day would start off on the exercise yard with the physical training instructor going through his vigorous fitness routine. If they wished, some of the fitter and more energetic staff could join in; few did, especially in the winter months.

I would volunteer for night duties, because I was not yet living in married quarters (I was still awaiting a vacancy) and there was little difference sleeping in the centre or in my bachelor's pad. I also received a generous allowance for doing so and this extra cash went a good way to paying for my motorcycle, which was an ideal means of transport to commute between Rochdale and Bolton, some fourteen miles away.

I had carried out the duty of sleep-in at the gate many times, so I was well accustomed to the routine. Apart from having to call the doctor out on a very few occasions, the only other time I was disturbed from my sleep was when the Warden or his Deputy paid his monthly night visit, which was a Home Office regulation. On his arrival he would ring the front door bell and the sleep-in gate officer would dress in full uniform and answer the front door. The door would then be unlocked, but still retained on a very strong chain. The Warden would be identified and asked if he was alone. If there was someone else with him, the Warden would introduce the visitor and I would ask to see his or her official Home Office pass.

No pass in effect meant no entry for either of them. Yes! The basic grade officer can tell the Warden that he is not permitted to enter his own establishment. On only two occasions was a visitor accompanied by the Warden not allowed to enter the establishment. One of them was a very famous Member of Parliament.

On New Year's Eve, the prison had been fully secured and I telephoned my wife to wish her a happy New Year.

I had been on duty for twelve hours so it was time to lock myself in the 'sleep-in room' and go to sleep which did not take long. I had just gone into a deep sleep when the alarm bell rang and my telephone rang. It was the night orderly officer, he said, "One of the night patrol officers has informed me that he can smell something burning."

I told him that I would ring the fire brigade. I put the telephone down and then dialled 999. I said to the operator, "Fire at Buckley Hall detention centre, in what place we do not know yet, all inmates will be unlocked and will be located on the parade ground, all doors will be unlocked. You will have free access to anywhere."

Why was I so efficient? Because the fire emergency orders on the procedure board (in bold print) were on the wall, just above the telephone. I unlocked the main entrance, then went up into the dormitories, and helped the orderly officer and the night patrol staff to awaken all the trainees and to muster them all on the parade ground. One or two were difficult to arouse, but the shouting of, "Fire - fire!" soon got them to their feet. I do admit that several had the contents of their water jugs poured over their heads; some needed a gentle slap. Every trainee was ordered to take a couple of their blankets outside with them; this would help them to keep warm.

After all it was 1 January. Overall, everything went to plan; however, I did hear a few fucks, twats, and bastards.

By this time, it was obvious that the fire had started in the kitchen. From the exercise yard, we could now see the flames getting fiercer. We did a head count of our trainees, the orderly officer counted 100, and I counted 100. I said, "We are one short, shit!"

One trainee said, "Bottomley is in the hospital."

I said, "Christ! So he is."

The orderly officer shot off like a greyhound and retrieved the poor sod. Later, the orderly officer told me that Bottomley was fast asleep when he had got to the hospital. Everyone was now feeling the cold.

By this time, the sirens of the fire engines, police and ambulances, could be heard in the distance, becoming louder and louder as they all got closer to the centre. The Warden and extra staff had arrived. The orderly officer reported that all the trainees and staff had been accounted for.

The Governor said, "Well done; now we have to get Bottomley to hospital, and find somewhere to send these poor freezing sods. I want them away from here as soon as possible."

The Warden said to the senior police officer, "Have you any ideas inspector? Manchester is too far and I realize you cannot put them all in your nick at Rochdale, but they must go somewhere that is warm, sod the security."

The fire was well under control, in what seemed minutes. The fire brigade's well-planned preparation and practice had paid off. About twenty minutes later fleets of black police vans arrived and all the trainees were loaded into the vehicles and taken to all the police stations in the area, some even went into a local community centre; every trainee was provided with a hot meal, and a nice cup of tea. Next day they were all transferred to various penal establishments. On the orders of the Home Office, many trainees that were nearing the end of their sentences were sent to their homes. The Warden called it compassionate remission.

I was put in charge of the farm party, therefore a new drill instructor had been found. A new officer by the name of Barker, an ex-guardsman, took my place. He was good; I shall leave it at that.

The farm was manned by inmates who could be trusted to work outside on the farm, with the minimum of supervision.

I took to this type of work straight away. Off with the uniform jacket and hat, overalls on, and I got stuck in. I will always remember the first day I took the farm party to the farm.

We had to go via a public road, which was the main access road to the Centre for vehicles. I told the inmates to get into line, hands out of pockets; I then ordered a 'quick march' and marched them the half-mile to the farm.

Having all gone through my drill instruction at some time or other, the inmates were just like guardsmen, marching past the church, I was really proud of them, not one had complained. After a full day's work I marched all of them back to the centre. On the way, back the Warden was going off duty in his car.

As he passed I ordered, "Eyes right - eyes front." The lads carried out the order, one or two laughed (quietly).

Next day the Warden called me into his office.

The Warden said, "That was a very good display yesterday Officer Smith, but too much bullshit, I know you mean well and I was impressed; but we must tone it down a little. I mean, keep them together, but no marching. I do hope you understand." Obviously, I had been over zealous.

Some time later one trainee suggested that it would be quicker to get to the farm if we went over the fields. Later I put this suggestion to the Warden who agreed. As time passed it became acceptable for the trainees to go to the farm without escort, which meant that I could go straight from my home, near the farm; then phone the centre to confirm they had all arrived, the reverse procedure was adopted for the return journey. It worked a treat until four of them decided to try to catch the bus to Manchester. They were soon rounded up at the bus station, by staff and police. Then it was back across the fields, with me escorting them from now on.

I had become very interested in farming and gardening, especially the livestock side of farming.

When a vacancy for a deputy 'farm and gardens' officer at HM Young Offenders Centre at Aylesbury, Buckinghamshire came up, I thought, 'What a great opportunity for the family and myself; what a lovely part of England.' I submitted my application and was successful. I discussed the move with Jeanie and the kids and it was 'Aylesbury here we come!' I had made many friends at Buckley Hall. It had made me a far better and more mature person.

Terry Newman, Ernie Foster, Bill Carmichael (the Warden) and I had in three years taken our staff table-tennis team from the third division to the first. We had won every league title and several knockout cups. We were, along with Bill Carmichael, responsible for the Rochdale and District Championships being held annually at Buckley Hall. This was an annual event very much appreciated by the local community and the inmates.

Our staff/inmate soccer team was unbeatable; one of the main reasons for this is that we were forced to play all out fixtures at home, for obvious reasons.

Just before I was transferred to Aylesbury our Warden was replaced by a new Warden. This man will remain nameless because he rocked the boat, putting an end to all the sporting activities with the local community and treating the establishment like Colditz. These changes of attitude and routines upset the apple cart and I was pleased that I was leaving.

My family and I had a good farewell party and we received many gifts, including flowers for my wife and a pewter mug for me. Buckley Hall had been very good to my family and me; it had provided a solid base for all the family to face up to the future. I was now an officer with five years experience behind me.

Chapter 10
HM Young Prisoners Centre Aylesbury

I arrived in the small market town of Aylesbury by train; it is only approximately forty miles north of London. What a contrast from Manchester from where I had just caught my train. Just two rail tracks, surrounded by a few buildings with green countryside and many beautiful trees. I took a taxi to the prison, good job I did, because Aylesbury prison was over a mile away and I had two suitcases to carry. The official name of the prison: Her Majesty's Young Prisoners Centre.

The prisoners were referred to as Young Prisoners, YPs for short. Prisoners aged from 15 to 21 years of age. Once attaining the age of 21, these prisoners would be transferred to an adult prison.

Aylesbury prison is a very old prison. Built in the late eighteenth century, in the past it has been used for long-term male prisoners and for female prisoners. The great train robbers were held in the hospital wing of the prison for the duration of their trial.

Over this long period, many executions took place inside the prison and many public hangings took place outside of the prison in years long gone by. When I arrived, I was shown the simple graves of those who had been executed; in those days all those who were hanged were buried in the grounds of the prison. That was the law in those days.

The hangman's scaffold was still in its original position. It was constructed of solid oak and it was a work of art. I was allowed to test the trap door; it was still in very good working order. Just to see if it was in good working order I tested it using a sand bag, it worked very well indeed.

There were two prisons contained within the high walls of Aylesbury prison. The main prison was built in the shape of a wheel, without the rim, not unlike the shape of an asterisk. All wings led to the centre, from where the prison was controlled. Each wing was three storeys high; each storey's landing contained forty cells, twenty on each side the landing. There were latrines, and wash basins in the middle of each landing. The five wings were named A, B, C, D and E. These wings were used for YPs sentenced to medium and long-term sentences, ranging from eighteen months to life. The main prison was run on a grading system. We also had an Induction wing, located above the Reception wing; both of these wings were attached to 'A' wing by an annexe. 'A' wing had very easy access to the main gate. Therefore, this was the best place to receive and discharge prisoners.

After going through the reception routine, each YP was located on the Induction wing, where they received a thorough medical examination, a simple IQ test, and their prison record (documents) was started.

Induction staff interviewed each YP and wrote a simple assessment on each of them. In short, it was a way of us getting to know them and for the prisoners to get to know us. They were also informed of the prison rules and what was to be expected of them. Their EDR

(Earliest Date of Release) and LDR (Latest Date of Release) were calculated. They were told of this, the details being entered into their records.

In those days, they could earn up to one-third off their sentence in remission for good conduct; it is now fifty percent, far too much in my opinion.

From Induction they would be located on the wing best suited for the job they had been allocated. Those selected for the kitchen and library would be located on 'A' wing. Young prisoners are allocated work in the laundry and the many other types of workshops; all would be housed and located on 'B' wing. By good conduct and industry all YPs who met the criteria could progress to 'C' wing. This wing allowed extra privileges, including more association time, table-tennis, and a communal TV. Most of the 'Red-Bands' (prisoners who can be trusted) were located on 'C' wing which had a far more relaxed regime; misbehave and it was back to 'B' Wing!

The other prison was referred to as 'F' and 'G' Wings. Comprising two wings that ran parallel with each other, these wings housed the very long-term prisoners, the prisoners who were serving life sentences - HMP (Her Majesty's Pleasure) and long-term indeterminate sentences, those who had no fixed date of release.

For the vast majority, this was their first custodial sentence. Sorry but true, but there were at least 90 such prisoners. Obviously, the regime had to be more relaxed. Each YP had their own cell and spent most of the day and evenings either on educational classes or in specialist workshops.

We even had a workshop that compiled books in Braille for the blind. This workshop was once the topic of a National TV programme. Throughout my twelve years I spent at Aylesbury, I had very little dealings with 'F and G Wing'.

We also had a very well equipped Hospital wing and the 'Choky', the slang name for the Punishment wing. Yes! Prisoners were punished; bread and water had long since stopped being implemented, yet it still remained on the Governor's list of punishments.

I was soon introduced to Mr Fletcher (the Governor) and to Mr Cowling (the Chief Officer). Both had been in the prison service for many years and I soon found out just how well these two men organised their staff and the prisoners.

The prison was very clean. All staff knew their duties and God help an officer or YP who stepped out of line. It was all run on 'military style' discipline and it was a very well organised prison.

Staff saluted their superior ranks and all officers had to declare the number of prisoners that they had in their charge. It was a proper prison.

I had been posted here to take charge of the garden party, responsible for the maintenance of the entire gardens and lawns inside the prison. Every other weekend I would be in charge of the farm, this was a pig-fattening unit.

There were also two full-sized soccer pitches and a cricket square to prepare and maintain. It is said that the wicket was the best batting wicket in the whole of Buckinghamshire. Well, that is what I thought.

My boss, the Farm Officer Instructor, was named Wally Dell. He was also responsible for the maintenance of the prison officers' quarters' area and the maintenance of the Governor and Deputy Governor's gardens.

All the prisoners who worked on the farm were within a few months of their release date, or were all trusted to conform. One misdemeanour and they would most likely lose remission, finish back on 'B' wing, and would never be allowed to work outside ever again. All the prisoners thought working outside a 'perk' and very few abused that privilege.

It is a fact that some of the prisoners, especially from the London area, had never even seen a pig before in the whole of their lives. Having two good stockmen working on the pig unit was very important. This would allow you to keep an eye on those working well away from the farm. I used a tractor when keeping a check on them.

The farm was a pig-fattening unit only. My boss, Wally Dell had served in the Royal Navy, a man who had been a prison officer instructor on farms for many years. He knew how to control prisoners; he stood no nonsense from anyone, especially young prisoners. Wally knew his job and was keen to share his knowledge with me. I soon became aware of the skills needed. It made the job easier because I was 100 percent interested in my work.

With the cheap labour and the waste food from the prison, the farm made a very good profit for the Prison Department. When Wally was off duty, I would cover for him. I soon became quite a knowledgeable gardener, grass mower and became very interested in the pig unit. The outdoors was very healthy employment; it was ideal work for the prisoners.

My house (quarter) was next to the farm. Opposite there was an orchard, with large open fields for my fast-growing children to play in. A new addition was born in Aylesbury. Duncan was born in 1972, just three years after I had left Rochdale.

My eldest son David was now twenty, a big strong lad who was playing rugby for the Aylesbury 'B' team. He played guitar and did regular gigs in pubs and clubs, all that Donavon stuff, all right in moderation, but not morning, noon, and night.

Don junior had started work as a toolmaker and Donna was a shop assistant at Woolworth's. Sue and Barbara were still at school. Jeanie my wife certainly had her work cut out. It was at about this time that Wally Dell left to go to Her Majesty's Prison 'The Verne', which is in Dorset.

I took over the management of the farm and all the garden instructors. I missed Wally Dell. He had not been just a good boss, but a very good friend. He had been promoted and returned back to his home county of Dorset. My new partner, who was to take over my old job on the 'inside gardens', was Officer Instructor 'Nobby' Clark from Her Majesty's Prison Lewes. A very different man from Wally, but a man I came to admire and respect.

Nobby was very quiet man, who got on with his job, with the minimum of fuss.

A very clever man, but a man I thought should never have been a prison officer, not because he could not do the job, but because he was just too nice a person. He was about ten years older than I was; he had forgotten more about gardening than I would ever know.

He had been in the service far longer than me, and had been a gardening instructor for many years. He was fully qualified to instruct the inmates in horticulture on evening classes in the prison. A very nice, very quiet man, who I thought could have some difficulty controlling the inmates; my thoughts were soon dispelled when he took

over my party and sacked the lot. He then went round
the wings interviewing prisoners who he thought would
be interested and more suitable.

I had always received prisoners for the party on the
recommendations of other officers. Nobby's system
seemed to have worked, because he always put on a good
garden display and had little trouble from his prisoners.
His evening classes were very popular and very well
attended. His only failing was that he knew absolutely
nothing about pigs.

He would soon learn, because he was as keen as
mustard.

I was the boss of the farm now. I took between fifteen
and twenty prisoners to the farm every day of the week,
with the exception of Saturday and Sunday, when only
the stock lads would be working.

I would mark out the soccer fields myself. I was in
contact with the Centre Principal Controller by both
telephone and radio.

Livestock command a seven-day week. Two trusted,
well-trained prisoners looked after the hundred or so
pigs; the rest maintained the sports fields and the officers'
quarters including the Governor's gardens. It was a good
life, and I was never happier than when I was on the
farm.

Due to staff shortages, I did have to cover discipline
duties in the prison in the evenings and on my weekends
off. I could work eighty hours a week with ease. I was
becoming rather prosperous in a small way. I had bought
my first car and my wife and I enjoyed a good social life.

At about this time Susan, aged seventeen, had left the
flock to live with her future husband Chris. I was hurt at

the time but I had to accept it, the world was changing and the old-fashioned standards had gone.

My world fell apart when David my eldest son was arrested for being in possession of cannabis. He had been mixing with bad company and had become hooked on the weed. Sadly this led on to him using the hard stuff and several prison sentences followed. I tried very hard to get him to change and get his self-destructing habit under control, but alas, Jeanie and I failed. His lovely wife left him and took their two children with her. David had become a heroin addict. I did visit him in various prisons.

My Governor and Chief Officer were sympathetic and always made my visits to the various prisons 'private'. In fairness to David, he never once gave my address when he was in trouble. He had broken my heart. (As I write, David is 51 and a grandfather). He has lost his family, his health, and his dignity; however, he is still our son, and his mother and I still love him. What a waste of a life, not only has it ruined his life but his addiction has affected all the family.

I expect him to depart this world before I do. He now lives in Aylesbury; he is a very sick man. His son and daughter tend to his needs when he is in his purpose-built flat. Regretfully he now spends more time in hospital than he does in his home. He accepts what mistakes he has made, but it is far too late to put the clock back. My mind sometimes goes back to the days when he was that great big, healthy fullback and playing rugby up there in Lancashire with my parents watching him play; how proud we all were.

Most of his peers are dead, some passing away in their late teens or early twenties. I am still in touch with him, but not often enough; he has little or no contact with any of his brothers and only his sister Sue sees to his needs. He does see his two children and grandson far more often now; but he leads a very lonely life. He still plays the guitar and reads a lot. He is content in his own way I suppose. What might have been? What a waste?

(Note added later - As I wrote this book David passed away after years of painful suffering. He died on 5 November 2003, aged 51 years old. RIP.)

Two young prisoners who had been charged with IRA offences were located at Aylesbury. Big changes had to be made. A very secure fence was erected all around the farm. All movement of the livestock and all goods vehicles had to be reported to 'Security Control'. My labour force was cut from about twenty prisoners to three, then down to two.

I informed the Governor that it was impossible to manage the farm without adequate labour.

He said, "The farm will have to go. Aylesbury Prison has been designated a category 'A' prison."

I tried to save the farm, but deep down I knew I would not win. It just was not practical. Within days, I took all the pigs to the slaughterhouse. I was very sad.

I returned to discipline duties because all I was left with was a now unused pig unit, and I did not fancy spending the rest of my service mowing the grass on the sports fields. When the livestock went, so did my interest.

The time had come to move on. I reverted from Officer Farm Instructor to Basic Grade Officer, so I was back to where I had started all those years ago. Having been working evenings and at weekends in the prison, I did have the knowledge of how to carry out my new duties. Being senior to most officers, by the length of service I had served, I was detailed by the Wing Principal Officer to work on 'B' two landing. Two officers ran the landing when the prisoners were on the wing, each officer covering one half of the landing. Being the most senior, I was in charge of the landing.

Being a good prison officer is getting to know the prisoners in your charge, so you more or less did everything those thirty or so prisoners did. If they went to work, you took them there, if they went to shower or to change their clothes, as their landing officer you would go with them. You read their outgoing and incoming mail, and you submitted a monthly progress report to the Wing Principal Officer to help him to assess the prisoners for labour changes and most important of all, home-leave and parole.

The landing officer was the main link to upper management.

The principal officer was in charge of the wing, assisted by the senior officer who besides assisting the principal officer would be in charge of number one landing.

With a full complement of staff, there would normally be a minimum of two officers on each landing. You soon got to know the prisoners in your care, even down to knowing each prisoner's individual prison number, who they wrote to, who - if anyone - cared for them on the outside. The landing officer played a major role in the progress or otherwise of a prisoner. I soon got back into the swing of being a 'Basic Grade Officer'.

My weekend and evening overtime had put me in good stead and my time at the Detention Centre proved time well spent. I had now been a prison officer for about ten years; it was time I was looking for promotion. First, you must pass the Principal Officers Promotion Examination, not an easy examination to pass, unless you did some studying, pleased the right people and your face fitted.

One day the Principal Officer called me into his office and told me that his 15-year-old son had been caught stealing bottles of beer from the local pub; the other lad had not been apprehended.

His son would not disclose the other lad's name.

I said to the Principal Officer, "That's what you call loyalty."

The PO bawled, "Loyalty my backside He should tell the police the other lad's name."

I asked, "What would be gained by that?"

The PO said, "They should share the blame."

I replied, "Then your son would be called a grass."

The PO bawled, "Bullshit!"

I left the office thinking it was not the end of the world; I couldn't understand why he was making such a great issue of such a minor thing.

I went off duty for my evening meal. All the family ate together and we always enjoyed my wife's cooking. Dave my eldest son was not his usual boisterous self.

I asked, "You look down in the dumps Dave, anything the matter?"

Dave replied, "Yes dad, I have been pinching beer from the 'County Arms' with Steve. Steve got caught; I want to give myself up."

"Well my boy if that is what you want to do you must do it, get it off your chest, you will feel better. I will go down to the police station with you; a very foolish thing to do, but thank you for being honest."

We went down to the local police station and young David made a statement. The constable said he would submit the details of my son's statement to his superior. Next day at the prison I told the Principal Officer that it was my son David, who was the other lad who had stole the beer from the 'County Arms' with his son Steve.

The Principal Officer bawled, "I knew it, how many times have I told Steve not to mix with your son? He's trouble!"

Now this was getting personal so I suggested we discuss the matter in private.

The PO said, "No! This is as good as place as any."

I said, "OK! But we do not pull rank; my son David admitted to me of his own free will. He also had the guts to go to the police and inform them of his part in this matter; which when all is said and done was wrong, but it was only a boyish prank. Remember your lordship; it was your stupid son that got caught."

I should not have said that. I knew I had said far too much, but it had to be said, it takes two to tango.

I said, "I've said enough on the issue so I shall go. If it goes to court, I shall stand by my son; I suppose it will be too far above your station to do the same?"

I had to work with this principal officer for the next two years. I could have asked for a move to another wing, but that is not my style.

I did pass my promotion examination, but this principal officer always took our past exchange of words personally. It was he who wrote my annual report and everyone knew the reason why I was always knocked-back for promotion. Both our lads received a caution from a police inspector; it never went to court.

As I write this now, my next eldest son Don is the Senior Training Officer for a very large national company, married with two grown-up daughters.

One of his daughters, Debbie, has just completed a degree at university.

Young Steve, David's mate, sadly committed suicide at the age of 26. As for my favourite principal officer (young Steve's father), he attained the rank of Chief Officer, but sadly died in his mid-fifties from a heart attack. May they both RIP, I sincerely mean that.

As I have written previously what counted most amongst staff in the prison service, was seniority. Seniority! I have even heard officers arguing over seniority as the difference in the number of days that they have been in the service, but at the end of the day it is the senior basic grade officer who carries the can if anything goes wrong.

There were eighty to ninety Young Prisoners on each of the four wings, four landings on each wing, on average just over 300 in total in the main prison. We did try to ensure that each prisoner had a single cell to himself. A good prison officer must understand that all prisoners have good days and bad days, they have mood changes; they get depressed and some get homesick. Showing a little sympathy and understanding at the right time can save a great deal of heartache and save an officer from getting a punch on the nose, which did happen from time to time.

If you kick your dog every day, one day it will turn and bite you, not that I never saw a prisoner kicked, punched, or badly treated at Aylesbury. The Governor,

Chief Officer, and all the staff at Aylesbury can all hold their heads up high. I was at Aylesbury Young Prisoners Centre for just under twelve years.

It was a pleasure to serve there. It also allowed me to bring my ever-increasing family up in a healthy, trouble free environment. Well, that is what I thought at the time.

The years passed so quickly and my children were now teenagers, with the exception of Duncan who was still a toddler.

Since the arrival of the two young IRA prisoners, the Maguire brothers, one aged 16 and the other one aged 19, Aylesbury had become a top security (Category 'A') prison. Security had been increased and there was a different atmosphere, both amongst the prisoners and staff. Far less privileges, and less time out of their cells, made the regime far too rigid.

The farm and pigs had long gone and the beautiful sports fields were seldom used. Gone was the staff's annual fête we used to put on for the people of Aylesbury and the towns and villages for miles around. One year we had the RAF motorcycle team; Charlie Drake once paid us a visit. It was a very well organised fête and this was mostly due to the splendid efforts of senior works officer Ken Dorrington.

All this had come to an end, because two young lads had been sentenced to five years' detention for allegedly being members of the IRA and being involved in the blowing up of a pub. It had been a dastardly crime. Management had been right to upgrade security. I was still on 'B' wing, 2 landing and this is where the two young IRA prisoners where located.

Although brothers they were not allowed to share a cell (it is fair to say that very few prisoners shared cells at Aylesbury). However, they were very lucky to be on the same landing in cells next to each other.

Over the weeks I had come to know these two young men very well. Always smart and respectful, never any problems from them, they were very well-behaved prisoners. When censoring a prisoner's mail you read between the lines. Both their parents, along with an uncle of the Maguires, had been given long custodial sentences for their alleged contacts with the IRA.

The letters they received from their parents, especially the ones from their mother, only contained references to all the family's innocence and giving her sons hope and encouragement. After months of getting to know these young men and their family, I was convinced they had never conspired with any terrorist organisation. They were not guilty of any criminal offences. It was a very well-documented fact that prisoners with IRA connections always received the 'IRA Monthly Newsletter'.

The young Maguires never received any such newsletters.

Many years later whilst I was serving at Her Majesty's Prison Parkhurst, the headlines in all the national newspapers reported that all the Maguire family had been set-up by false police evidence. On the basis that false forensic evidence had been produced at the original trial, the Court of Appeal had no alternative but to uphold the appeal and to release the Maguires. The lads, now adults, had already served their full sentences, and were back working in society. Their parents had served over ten years, now freedom at last for them also. Alas, it was far too late for their uncle; he had died whilst in prison.

I wish all the family well, albeit a little late.

Governments and judges find it impossible to accept that the police and the judiciary sometimes get things wrong. There is a lot of evidence to support this. There are hundreds of prisoners in the penal systems that are innocent.

I had now moved from 'B' 2 landing to 'B' 1 landing and was assisting the wing Senior Officer Roy Ashcroft. Thankfully, the Principal Officer was carrying out many other duties such as acting Chief Officer or Orderly Officer whose job it is to ensure the smooth running of the whole prison. We saw very little of our Wing Principal Officer, thank God! Although, a good officer he was such a big-headed, unsociable snob, who still only spoke to me when he had to do so. Our two sons were now at loggerheads, and he always took things personally. When Roy acted up to Principal Officer Duties, I was made up to Acting Senior Officer. At last! A step in the right direction, although I knew as long as my regular Principal Officer was writing my annual reports, I would never gain promotion.

One evening I was sitting in my office, finalising the locking up reports when I heard a noise from the outside.

I ordered an officer to keep his eye on things for me and I told him that I was going to have a quick look outside.

I got a torch from the Centre Principal Officer and told him I had heard a noise. The PO said, "That bloody barn owl again I bet."

I went to the wall that my office was located on. Starting at one end of the wing, I pointed the beam from the torch to the ground where it joins the wall. I was looking for brick dust; this is the best method of detecting if a prisoner is trying to make a hole in the outer wall of his cell.

He can easily get rid of the dust in his cell and fill or cover it with something. This method was much quicker than searching every cell, although a search of the outside walls, locks, bolts and bars is made every day by the landing officer. The officer must sign that this has been carried out in the 'Locks, Bolts and Bars' book.

About ten yards from my office I saw fresh, powdery brick dust on the ground. Shining the beam of the torch upwards, I saw a couple of feet and legs dangling from the cell wall. I raised the alarm by blowing my whistle continually, until the outside patrols arrived. I returned inside the prison and went straight to the cell that 'Houdini' was (half) occupying. On unlocking the door the prisoner said, "Thank God you found me Mr Smith, it's a long drop down there and my arse is stuck."

He was taken down to the punishment wing. Some days later he was awarded 56 days loss of remission and located in a more secure cell. Now classified, an escapee, he would wear yellow stripes on his trousers and a yellow patch on his jacket. He would never again be unsupervised. Later on when he became 21, he was transferred to her Majesty's Prison Wakefield.

I had been on 'B' wing for just over two years. It was time to move on. The Chief told me that I was now an official Acting Senior Officer.

One day the Chief Officer called me into his office and said, "Don, I want you to take charge of the Induction Wing."

I had always got on with the Chief; we played darts for the prison team and were both keen on cricket. Had anyone else been present he would have referred to me as Officer Smith.

It was sad to be leaving 'B' wing; I was leaving some good mates. However, I was looking forward to my new job. I was to take charge of the Induction Wing. A new job, a new challenge, and a new Principal Officer would be writing my annual reports; that would be a bonus in itself.

Whilst I have already referred to the Induction Unit previously I do think it worth while to refresh your memories. The Induction Unit received the prisoners as soon as they had gone through their reception routine.

The main function of the Induction Unit was to try to assess each prisoner.

They received a full medical examination, were interviewed by the Education Officer and the Psychiatrist and would later be accessed by the Physical Training Instructor. We carried out simple IQ tests and wrote a brief report on what we expected of them; we were not always right. We asked them what sort of work they would prefer whilst in the prison; obviously those wanting to sweep the roads outside the prison did not get their wish. In short, it was a couple of weeks spent on getting to know them and them getting to know us, the routines, rules and what we expected of them. In my opinion, it was two weeks well spent. After two weeks they were located into the main prison wings, which the induction staff had thought best suited their needs; the time spent with us had given them a chance to acclimatise and to get to know just what to expect.

One day I had just located a prisoner to his designated wing and I was informing the receiving officer of some details about the prisoner. I saw a prisoner who I knew as Mack coming towards us carrying a thick sweeping brush handle; Mack was swearing and shouting as I went over to meet him. I said, "What's the matter, Mack?"

Then without warning he started to beat me about the head, arms, and legs with the brush handle. I tried to fend him off, but one of the blows to my head had made me feel groggy and sickly. I remember going to the floor, and could hazily see staff running to my assistance. I remember being helped to my feet and a party of prisoners on their way to the gym all appeared to be grinning.

I was taken to Stoke Manderville Hospital where my head, arms, and legs were X-rayed. Thankfully, no bones had been broken, but I did feel terrible.

I was kept in overnight and released the next day; it was then straight to bed. My pride had been hurt more than my body.

In over twelve years of service, that was the first time I had been seriously assaulted. But why had Mack decided to attack me? We had always been on reasonable terms. I was off duty on sick leave for about ten days.

When I returned to the prison the first thing I did was go to the segregation unit to see Mack, I wanted to know why he had attacked me.

In company with two other officers, I visited Mack in his cell.

I said, "Mack, why did you attack me like you did?"

Mack said, "I am very sorry Mr Smith, I do not know why; I just flipped my lid and I am very sorry, please forgive me."

I told Mack that he would be charged with GBH and would receive more time.

Mack said, "Yes! I know and I deserve it."

Mack appeared at Aylesbury Crown Court and was sentenced to a further six-month term of imprisonment, to run consecutively with his present four-year sentence: that means six months longer.

Mack was later transferred to Her Majesty's Prison Brixton straight from the court. The assault had hurt, but what had hurt me most was why it had happened.

I did lose a little confidence, but I soon got back into the routine and I was soon able to put the episode behind me.

Aylesbury only received long-term prisoners; we would only receive between six and twelve prisoners a week.

The reception unit was attached to our unit so I saw them come and I saw them go. You could say, sad and happy times. Being in charge of the Induction Unit had been the most interesting work since I had left the farm.

After nearly two years, I was aware my time in the Unit was drawing to a close. Maybe I would be detailed to serve on the Lifers' Wing or even go back to 'B' wing.

One Sunday I was walking across the exercise yard when the Governor called me over to him.

He said, "Officer Smith I have had notification by Head Office that you have been promoted to the rank of Senior Officer, as from today. You will be notified of your transfer in due course." He shook me by the hand and said, "Well done."

After seventeen years, I had gained recognition.

I could not wait to get home and tell Jean and the rest of my family. This promotion meant another move, also a big increase in my salary.

Where would we be sent? 'Not back up north,' I thought, the family would not like to do that, after the country style life we had all become accustomed to.

At dinner, we discussed all the possibilities, back up to the north of Birmingham, down to the West Country, or to the south? It was not a choice we could make; it was where the Department wanted me to go.

When I returned to duty, I was informed that the Governor wanted to see me. I knocked on the Governor's door, the Governor said, "Come in, hello! Senior Officer Smith, your posting has come through and they have decided to send you to London. How do fancy going to work at Her Majesty's Prison Wandsworth, London?"

'Christ!' I thought. 'What a bloody place to take my family? What would Jean and the kids say? God only knows!'

Chapter 11
Her Majesty's Prison
Wandsworth

I was very pleased to have been promoted, even though it had taken me seventeen years, however, I knew it would now mean very big changes to the lives of all my family. Decisions had to be made; we had to make plans about re-housing, new schools, and my youngest daughter Barbara, who had just started work in Aylesbury, had to seek new employment in the London area.

Donald and Donna were now married, living their own lives. Sue was still in her flat and was about to get married to Chris, a Cockney (nut case). Well that is what I thought at the time. He turned out to be a good lad, although the truth was I could not get used to the prospect of having an Arsenal supporter in the family, Chris was an Arsenal fanatic.

David my elder son had become more involved in drugs and had lost contact with his wife and his two lovely children; he was in and out of various prisons for drug-related crimes. He was now totally dependent on heroin. He had broken my heart, but life had to go on, I had the rest of my family to consider.

My wife and I now had six wonderful grandchildren. However, David was still our son and we visited him in all the various prisons he was sent to.

I made the move South. As I was going over Wandsworth Bridge in my car, I can remember saying to myself, 'What have I let myself in for?'

I stayed in digs, at an old lady's house, very near to the prison, until I had acquired a house, and then my family would join me. Wandsworth prison was a very old Victorian-built prison, large, murky and it gave me a feeling of depression. There were two prisons behind those high walls at Wandsworth; both prisons were in the shape of a cartwheel, without the rim.

The spokes of the wheel made up the Wings, five storeys high (landings) with the first landing being in the basement. Number two landing was at ground level, so to speak. All wings led to the Centre (the hub) from where the prison was controlled. How it was controlled was marvellous, I marvelled at just how organised everything worked, just like clockwork.

The Centre Principal Officer controlled both of the prisons. Every order came from him, including the sounding of the centre bell, a real bell, not like the one you ring on your front door. This large brass bell was used to carry out the movements of all prisoners. This bell could be heard from miles away and everyone responded to it at once. The bell's main function was to muster all staff to the centre as soon as possible.

There were usually about a thousand prisoners located in cells in the main prison. The main prison consisted of A, B, C, D and E wings, each wing having it is own individual function.

'A' wing was used for all the prisoners who worked in the kitchen; all the kitchen orderlies were located on number one landing, for easy access to the main kitchen. 'A' 2 landing housed the red-bands. Yes! They did actually wear a red-band on their jacket sleeve. 'B' and 'C' wings housed short - and medium-term prisoners.

The majority of these prisoners would staff all the various workshops. Each landing had a couple of orderlies, who kept the wing clean and tidy. 'D' wing housed all the long-term prisoners and those prisoners on the escape list who had yellow stripes on their trousers and a yellow patch on their jackets, back and front; as well as these, there was the Category 'A' prisoner, located on their own special landing, and I (cannot say which landing).

All these prisoners on this wing worked in the mailbag shop. All prisoners were under maximum surveillance at all times; security was of the highest priority; some prisoners were awaiting transfers to maximum security prisons. 'E' wing was used to house all those prisoners who were mentally unstable, drug addicts and those who, whilst not needing full-time hospital care, were supervised by basic grade officers and several trained hospital officers. All drop outs of society; what a total waste of human life.

The end of 'E' wing lead straight to the prison hospital buildings, therefore, help was always at hand if needed. 'E' 1 landing was used mainly as a segregation unit for prisoners who found the going tough. Many well-known (so-called) tough gangsters have spent time on 'E' one landing. One called Foster, would spend most of his sentence on 'E' wing, not because he was special, he was just disruptive and could not do his 'bird' (sentence).

He had to create trouble; he got satisfaction from being a nasty troublemaker.

The duties of a senior officer were very varied and interesting at this very over-crowded prison, over 1700 lived and worked in this Victorian relic. I soon got into the routine; it was a very harsh routine. The prisoners knew exactly what was expected of them and how to toe the line; the discipline was very tough, both for staff and prisoner.

Everything worked so smoothly; prisoners had to keep in a line when moving from A to B and in the workshops they had even to ask the permission of the shop officers just to go to the toilet. Yes! I have seen some so-called hard men asking permission to go to the toilet. I have seen them put an arm up in the air and say, "Please may I go to the toilet, sir?"

They had to conform to the very strict discipline; the alternative was the punishment wing, which would mean loss of remission or even restricted diet, or the loss of most privileges, such as no radio, no tobacco, and no canteen and in exceptional cases no library.

The staff at Wandsworth never bent the rules and I found it hard to accept this tough, sometimes inhumane regime, but it did work and the harsh regime made life for the staff and the prisoners very easy.

For most of the day, the majority of the prisoners were at work, only about six landing cleaners and orderlies on each wing were to be seen in the prison. Cleaners that could be trusted! Trusted! Up to a point, about as much as I could lift myself up whilst standing in a bucket.

I was attached to 'A' wing for the first twelve months. It was a very easy wing to run. Most of the prisoners worked in the kitchen, the prisoners' canteen, library, and other jobs where they were trusted to a certain degree.

The Principal Officer on 'A' wing was Victor Yates. What a character! He had spent most of his service at Wandsworth.

He would say, "Give them nothing Mr Smith, give them fuck all; any requests for extra letters to write to your loved ones see Mr Smith, he's a soft touch."

Victor had no heart, just a swinging brick, no feelings, and I think that was the reason we had very little trouble on the wing.

Of the 200 or so prisoners on the wing only a couple would queue to make a request when Victor was on duty. When he was on leave or on other duties and I was in charge of the wing, I definitely dealt with at least twenty more applications per day. Soft touch, maybe! But I did try to be humane. Not that Victor was inhumane; he was just the product of the old school. Vic was an ex-Desert Rat, who, I feel had left his heart in the Sahara desert.

The alarm bell rang! That means everything stops, and the Centre Principal Officer directs all staff to the location of the trouble. It was a fight between two prisoners on the exercise yard. The problem was soon sorted. The two offenders were bundled to the punishment wing. They would remain there until the Governor dished out the punishment, usually next day. Seven days loss of remission was the order of the day for fighting; double that if they gave the Governor any lip.

One day when I was supervising the prisoners on a daily, one-hour exercise period, and a prisoner shouted, "We are not leaving the yard; we want to complain about the food."

I radioed the Security Officer to inform him of just what the situation was. By this time about 300 prisoners had sat in the centre of the yard; this is what is called a 'sit-down-protest'.

The Security Principal Officer told all the prisoners to make their complaint in the usual, official manner.

The ringleader shouted, "Fuck off bastards."

The Senior Chief Officer, the number one Chief, arrived. He ordered all staff to leave the yard, everything went quiet; you could hear a pin drop. The Chief walked into the centre of the mob and said, "You have three minutes to start moving back to your wings or I will set the dogs on the lot of you."

About six dog handlers, with their dogs had positioned themselves at various entries to the yard. The Chief shouted in a very bold, loud voice, "Your three minutes starts from now."

He then walked from the middle of the yard to one of the exit gates, situated in the perimeter fence.

The majority of prisoners started to return to their cells. Twenty or so prisoners remained; with a minute left to go the Chief shouted, "Dog handlers take up your positions."

All the prisoners shot to their feet and left the yard.

The chief turned to me and said, "Take the names and numbers of the last six prisoners who left the yard, nick them (Governors report) for inciting a riot; take them down to the punishment block and the Governor will deal with the bastards in due course. You must never give in to these bastards Mister Smith. Give them fuck all, I was not bluffing Mr Smith, the dogs would have bit their arses, but I did feel sorry for the dogs though. Make out a full report for the Governor. No doubt he will have words with me about the dogs, but that's what we have the bloody animals for, isn't it young man?"

Principal Officer Yates was nearing retirement. He had served over thirty years; I was also due to leave 'A' wing.

I shall always remember Victor Yates. He was a hard man, yet fair; he worked to the book and never gave an inch to anyone. I once remember an assistant governor telling him that one of the toilet bowls was blocked-up in one of the wing toilets. Victor's face went red, and he bawled, "Fuck off you shit-bag and never come on my wing unless I give you permission."

The assistant governor was gob-smacked and made a hasty retreat.

Principal Officer Yates did retire after over thirty years' loyal and conscientious service. He received a great farewell and send-off in the prison officers club; he was later awarded the Imperial Service Medal.

My next post was in charge of the prisoners' canteen, what a job. Two officers and I had, over a five-and-a-half day period, to serve 1700 prisoners with their weekly shopping. Shopping! They had just about a minute each to do their shopping.

The canteen was the place where all the prisoners purchase their tobacco, sweets, and other sundries. I do not think I have ever worked as hard in all my life.

My favourite command:

'Your name and number, you have one minute to spend up, or save; how much do you want to save? Sign there.'

There was never any cash involved; it was all done from the pay sheets. I must have asked those questions a million times in the two years I was in charge of the canteen. We had one prisoner to assist us, Basil, the grey fox; Basil was a trusted prisoner. What a crafty devil he was. He maintained the stock on the shelves and made the tea and coffee. Seven or eight prisoners (all redbands), all safe and sound in their own little office, did all the accounting. All these prisoners were in prison for fraud and embezzlement, so it was no surprise to me just how good they all were at bookkeeping and accounting.

One Sunday I did a 100% check of all the prisoners called 'Smith' (on what we called the live cards), each prisoner had a card, which informed us where he was located, where he worked and when he was to be released. On this particular Sunday, I decided to check the cards covering the 'Smiths', cross-checking from the 'live cards' to the pay sheets. On completing my check, I found 28 prisoners who did not exist. (The general term for these prisoners that do not exist is 'ghosts'.)

I said nothing to anyone at the time, but I soon found out that our trusted canteen orderly Basil (the grey fox) was deeply involved. The grey fox would collect the goods when signed for by the prisoners who worked in the clerks' office.

I submitted my findings to the Governor, who passed my memorandum on to the Administration Officer.

I heard nothing for weeks. I carried on in the canteen doing my duties, as if nothing was amiss.

One evening whilst browsing through the shelves in the canteen, I came across a wooden box, about the size of a shoe box, inside was a thick wad of £10.00 notes; £153.00 to be exact. I had to confront the other prison staff regarding this discovery; they knew it was there all right.

It was the result of cheating the receptions on arrival.

I confronted the two officers concerned in the swindle.

One officer, officer 'D' said, "Do not worry about that, it is what we carry over to replace surplus stock."

(Cash is never used in prison canteen transactions). I had stumbled upon a fiddle.

When serving the new receptions (usually those on remand and not sentenced) these two officer had deliberately overcharged the new prisoners for their goods and retained the goods. It is obvious to me that a third party on the outside exchanged the surplus stock for cash. Why they kept their booty in the prisoners' canteen, I do not know; the only explanation I can offer is that if an unacceptable loss was made they had the cash on hand.

All ready to replace stock, thereby balancing the books.

All prison canteens carry a small amount of surplus stock to balance the stock, following the weekly stock check. It is usually kept separate from the main stock.

I was far from happy by what I had found. I told officer 'D' to purchase stock at once with the cash, and that I would declare the surplus stock the next time we had an Administrator's monthly audit. This I did and the Administration Officer accepted my explanation that the stock had amassed over several months, however, he was not fully convinced and I could sense he knew that something was amiss. I was pleased it had been stopped and was now out in the open. No officer was disciplined; however, both officers concerned were moved to other duties.

Later I was called in to see the Administration Officer and we discussed my memorandum that I had earlier sent to the Governor.

He said, "Yes! Mr Smith we had suspected that the clerks in the canteen had been on the fiddle, it goes on in most large prisons. This had been going on for many years, but the alternative is to use officers or civilian staff to do the accounting, and that would cost the department thousands of pounds."

I could not accept his reasoning or logic. I told the Governor this and I requested that the Governor remove me from canteen duties as soon as possible, also that he attached a note to my record outlining the reasons for this request. This he did; to ensure that all was above board, I also requested that the Chief Officer countersign the details in my record, this he did, willingly.

The Chief Officer said to me, "Mr Smith, I think you have opened a can of worms."

I then said, "Well they can all go fishing for all I care now."

I could not stand dishonesty in any shape. It was obvious that I had to go. They could not afford to replace all the crooks that were (cooking) the books.

The Chief informed me that I was being put in joint charge of 'H' wing. This wing was situated in the smaller of the two prisons; it also contained F and G wings.

The smaller F, G and H prison wings catered for all the prisoners on remand, those awaiting trial, or sentence.

All the prisoners located on 'H' wing were perverts; paedophiles and any other freaks that Mother Nature had created.

All were classified as Rule 43 (not allowed association with other prisoners). With a total of nearly 200 it was impossible to work within the confines of Rule 43.

So, they all had to mix together. Some were classified Rule 43/43. These had to be unlocked and associate in small groups, we even had one prisoner who was classified Rule 43/43/43. He had to be unlocked on his own, or the other perverts would have killed him, so horrific was the nature of his crimes.

In spite of my feelings, all these prisoners had to be treated humanely. Some staff showed their contempt for them, but they had to be told that all prisoners are in prison as a punishment, not to be punished. It was our job to protect them from each other. Those prisoners allowed out of their cell during the day sat on the lower landing sewing mailbags. They were placid and sheepish; yet, beneath this guise, they were some of the most evil beings on earth. Easy to handle, but it was impossible to understand the reasons as to why they had committed such vile crimes.

One day the prisoner on Rule 43/43/43 was being seen by the Governor on his daily rounds. As we left the cell, he spat at the Governor. The spit missed the Governor and caught me full in the face. I threw a right hand punch and caught the bastard right on his jaw; he went down like a log. I locked the cell door. I said to the Governor, "Governor Sir…?"

The Governor interrupted me and said, "I'd have hit him twice, do not apologise Mr Smith. Charge him with assault. I will place him on restricted diet for a day or two; that should dry his mouth."

Because I had been spat in the face, I had to attend the local hospital for HIV and AIDS tests for over six months. That pervert was the only prisoner I ever hit in over twenty years of service. I was very wrong to do so; it was however just a natural, impulsive response, a knee-jerk reaction. I was attached to 'H' wing for nearly two years. My superiors must have been satisfied. When the Rule 43 prisoners did have their daily hour on the yard, they would be hissed and ridiculed as they passed other prisoners or by prisoners in workshops. The prison had far too many prisoners and the prison was grossly overcrowded.

One day I had to inform a Rule 43 prisoner that the Governor wanted to see him. He was in the communal showers, a place I always tried to avoid. It was very steamy and as I made my way through the shower room, I could hear a Rule 43 prisoner telling several other fellow prisoners about the offence he had committed on a little boy. All four of them were masturbating as the story of filth was being told. I had to get out as quickly as possible my blood was boiling. I told the Governor that the prisoner concerned was not yet available. I lit up a cigarette and sat down, I had to restrain myself. Next day I charged all four with 'indecent exposure'.

The Governor took fourteen days remission off all the four perverts.

I have had much experience in dealing with perverts.

I am convinced that they are all freaks of nature. They have developed as perverts when in the womb; it is in their genes. Whilst in prison they have received every type of treatment known to man; drugs, electric shock treatment, castration and many forms of counselling. Yet, they are no sooner released (which I disagree with) than they are back in prison. That means another child's life will be possibly ruined. In some cases another will die or be the subject of a video nasty.

All the do-gooders can say what they want. I say this 'once a pervert always a pervert'. Lock them all up and throw away the key. Harsh yes! But who should we protect, the pervert or the child?

There is no death penalty, so the alternative is to lock them up for ever; unless someone can come up with a 100% cure which I very much doubt at this time.

What I do accept is that these perverts are mentally sick, the same as a deformed limb, or some other deformity. The pervert is formed in this way, and it is just the same as anyone who has any abnormality. Because their crimes are so horrific, it does make society hate and loathe them, which is only natural.

Some months later the Chief Officer told me that I had done the correct thing by requesting to come out of the canteen. He did not like how things were being run. To be blunt, the canteen was corrupt and sleazy. Five years later, Her Majesty's Prison Liverpool underwent a full-scale inquiry into the corruption and fraud in their prison canteen. Many officers were involved and some were severely reprimanded, some were even dismissed the service.

I had been on the 'perverts' wing for nearly two years now.

Every so often I would call into the canteen clerks' office over in the main prison, where the prisoners were still working their devious fiddles on the books. Just to remind them all, that Senior Officer Smith knew what had gone on, and was still going on, I would pop my head into their office and say, "If I was still in charge, I would keep my eyes on the ghosts, get the drift fellows?"

At the same time, I told the old grey fox to keep his guard up. They would all look at the floor; they fully understood what I was referring to.

Back to 'H' Wing, these perverts had no shame, and would perform unnatural sexual acts on each other given the slightest chance. On canteen days, the prisoners purchased as much petroleum jelly as they did tobacco.

All of them claiming it were for skin treatment. Well, it was if you think about it.

I always remember a young officer catching two prisoners having anal sex in the toilet. He charged them with buggery. (It was a very serious offence in those days.) When he was giving his evidence to the Governor, the Governor asked him what had brought their behaviour to his attention. Blushing like a cooked lobster the young officer said, "Sir, as I looked under the toilet door I could see both pairs of boots together, pointing in the same direction."

At this point the Governor, Chief, and I could not help but break out into a bout of uncontrolled laughter. The proceedings had to be curtailed. The room was cleared. We all returned to the adjudication room. Again, when the officer read his statement and came to the mention of the 'boots pointing in the same direction', we all started to laugh again. The Governor thumped his desk with his fist and said, "Enough is enough, I can see the funny side, but this is a very serious matter. We will proceed in a civilised manner. Clerk, you will commence taking notes after the mention of the word 'boots,' at this rate we will be here all day."

Funny! But at the time it was a very serious matter. I had to look at the floor until the evidence had been completed. Had my eyes caught the eyes of the Chief, it is certain we would both have started to laugh again. It was a very serious offence in the 1980s, how times have certainly changed, but not for the better I fear. HIV and AIDS now run rampant within our prisons.

Whilst on duty I was informed that my young son Duncan had been hit by a motorcycle on the pelican crossing, near to the prison and had suffered very serious head injuries. After months in hospital, we got him home, but he was a nervous wreck and he found it hard to carry on at school. He would not leave his mother's side.

The injury had also badly affected the position of his eyes and the other kids took the piss out of him; some started to bully him. I had to get him away from that school and the city environment; after all, we were country people at heart.

My youngest daughter Barbara had left the fold and was now living with her boyfriend in Tooting.

My young son was still having great difficulty settling in at school. The road accident had shattered his confidence; he had to cling to his mother everywhere he went. He would abscond from school and come home on his own. We certainly had a problem on our hands. His physical injuries had healed, but the shock and trauma had left a mental scar. I had to get him away from the big city into a more relaxed environment. Several psychiatrists saw him and all agreed that he needed a change of scenery and a fresh start. I went to discuss my problems with the Governor who listened sympathetically.

He then said, "I agree with you Senior Officer Smith, take a week's leave and come to see me on your return; I will see what I can be arranged."

I thought to myself, 'What a nice chap.' I took Duncan and my wife to Spain, for a week in the sun.

We came home from our week's stay in Spain and I returned to duty. I had only been in the prison a couple of hours when the Centre Principal Officer told me that the Governor wanted to see me as soon as possible.

I knocked on the Governor's office door; the Governor called, "Come in! I have been in touch with the Prison Welfare Officer and the Regional Director and both feel that a transfer would be beneficial for all of your family, I also agree."

I was shocked that the Governor had given the matter such high priority. After all, he did have nearly 2000 prisoners and 400 staff to look after. I just said I would go to the prison where the need was the greatest.

The Governor said, "Well, Senior Officer Smith how would you and your family fancy going to live on the Isle of Wight?" (I could have fallen off my chair.) Discuss it with your wife and let me know what you decide. It will be at public expense, so your visit to the island will count as a pre-visit; have a nice time."

That was in effect giving us a week's free holiday on the Isle of Wight. We would visit the island, book into a hotel, have a look around for a house, visit the schools, and have tours of the prisons and the areas around them. All this would be paid for at public expense.

The Governor had done me proud. I thanked him because I knew this move would greatly help Duncan on his way back to making a full recovery. Jeanie and I were very, very delighted, over the moon in fact.

Chapter 12
HM Prison Parkhurst

We all went over on the ferry from Portsmouth to Wooton Creek; this in itself was a very pleasant experience for us all. We booked into the George Hotel in the centre of Newport. It was a very old hotel, but the service and quality of the food was excellent. We spent a couple of days visiting all the well-known beauty spots. It is such a beautiful place; how lucky we have been. Comparing grimy old Bolton to the sunny Isle of Wight is not unlike comparing chalk with cheese. Looking back, we had never really settled into city life in London.

I had loved the work at Wandsworth and had learned a great deal. I had worked very long hours; I had hardly ever seen my family. I thought, now is a chance to take things easy; how wrong I was going to be proved.

We had selected a house close to Parkhurst Forest.

A semi-detached, it had large gardens, back and front. The school for Duncan was just across the road. Jeanie was over the moon, we all were. We all returned to London to prepare our move. I met with the Governor of Wandsworth and thanked him for all he had done; I also informed him of our plans. The Governor wished me the best of luck, and said he hoped we would soon settle in.

He then asked, "Which prison have you selected?"

I said, "I am not bothered, Parkhurst will do me fine."

A few days later I returned to the Isle of Wight to select the wall coverings and measure up for the carpets and curtains. The works department informed me that my house would not be ready for about six weeks; therefore, I had to fix the family up with temporary accommodation until our house was ready for us to move into. I found a caravan park on the banks of the river Medina. I rented a large caravan, which was closest to the river. Jean and Duncan joined me a few days later. Our daughter Barbara was staying in London to supervise the packing and to organise the final removal. She had decided to stay with her boyfriend, they had recently announced their engagement, and had planned to get married in about a year's time.

There are two other prisons on the Isle of Wight - Her Majesty's Prison, Camp Hill, which at the time only received category 'C' prisoners (who can be trusted to work outside the prison, with the minimum of supervision) and Her Majesty's Prison, Albany which takes in class 'B' prisoners (who need supervision and where escape should be made as difficult as possible).

Parkhurst prison came over as a great let down. Prison! Compared to the other prisons I had served at it was just a holiday camp, with a very high security fence. Containment was all that mattered, very little discipline amongst the prisoners or staff. I soon realised that I had not selected the prison that best suited me. I had made my bed so it was up to me to make the best of it. Anyway, Duncan and Jeanie loved it here.

I bought Duncan a German shepherd dog puppy. We called him 'Duke'. What a friend he became. Our trips in the forest were some of the best times of our lives. We went fishing. I bought a small boat to catch the bigger fish. Living on the Isle of Wight was paradise and Duncan soon became well again.

I worked long hours, the money was good, but on reflection, I know now I was not seeing enough of my family. My mother and father came to stay with us every year; my children and my grandchildren were also regular visitors.

I always appeared to be on duty. Such were the staff shortages that I could be on duty for an extra thirty to forty hours a week.

Once whilst on night duty I calculated that over a twenty-one year period, (on the basis of working a forty-hour week) I had worked the equivalent of over seven years in overtime. This cannot be good for man or beast.

The Isle of Wight was such a lovely place to live, wide-open spaces, and the third largest forest in the UK to play in. You would never for one minute think that also living on this island were some of the wicked men in the whole of the United Kingdom.

My first job at Parkhurst was in the 'Emergency Control Room' (ECR). I was in charge of five officers and it was our function to organise and control all prisoner, vehicle and staff movements. The ECR staff also controlled the movement and security of the prisoners located in the 'Special Security Block' (SSB). Prison officers operated the Special Security Block.

I do not intend to discuss the security of these units for obvious reasons.

I must confess that when I went to be in-charge of the Emergency Control Room, I did not know the daily routine of the prisoners' movements. I also did not know the general layout or routines of the prison. I had been thrown in at the deep end. I, who was in charge, did not have a clue. The staff in the ECR understood this and helped me tremendously.

Officers Beck, Price, Long, Crane and Full, I them a belated, 'Thank you'!

I must be honest; I could not get to grips with all the sophisticated security gear; a fish out of water. I dropped a strong hint to the Chief Officer that the Emergency Control Room would be more efficient if I was re-allocated to other duties or until such time that I got to know the layout of the land and the routines of the prison.

I was soon transferred to the Special Security Block. (SSB)

I am far better working with prisoners. Inside the Special Security Block were some of the most notorious prisoners in the whole of the United Kingdom.

A principal officer, two senior officers, and twelve officers covered the unit, working on shifts. The principal officer spent very little time in the unit. He was just a figurehead; after he had completed his routine early morning inner fence check, he would then attend the Heads of Departments meeting, passing on all the information that the senior officers had provided him with. The senior officers ran the unit, working split shifts. During the night, a single officer operated the unit. He had no access to the prisoners. (It was not a job for the faint-hearted).

The staff working the night shift in the ECR and the CCTV cameras also monitored the SSB unit.

Just before I had started my duties in the Special Security Block one of the infamous prisoners had dropped dead from a massive heart attack.

His name was Sinman and he was only 45 years of age. He had gained his notoriety for his illegal drug empire. He had been operating his drug dealings mainly from Australia and in most countries in the Mediterranean area. He had married an Australian lawyer and had a young son. At the time of his death, his estate was said to be worth several million pounds sterling.

I soon settled into the routine of the SSB, and I enjoyed the work. The main emphasis was on security, and the prisoners realised that any chance of escape was all but a dream. That having been said, even the tightest security in the world can break down if staff become complacent or negligent. It was the senior officer's job to ensure that this did not happen. I must say that the vast majority of staff who worked in the SSB fully understood what a breach of security could lead to. Questions would be asked in the House of Commons, heads would roll.

Prisoners being held in the SSB during my period on duty there included Neilson, the 'Black Panther', who had murdered two sub-postmasters, and kidnapped and murdered Miss Leslie Whittle. He was definitely a psychopath, a wicked, evil monster. This prisoner was the strangest prisoner I had ever met, on making a request for a letter or to purchase paints for his artwork, he would write everything down, just in the style of a letter. He was so well organised and you could set the time of your watch by his preciseness.

In the Special Security Block, the seven to ten prisoners housed there had nearly every facility at their disposal. They had their own fully equipped gym and about three quarters of an acre of outside recreational land. This included a tennis court, which could be converted to a five-a-side soccer area. Some prisoners opted to have a garden or vegetable plot, a small greenhouse was also provided. Inside the building were a woodwork shop, TV and video room, and a small snooker table. Yes! I am talking about a prison. One must consider that most of these prisoners were serving multiple life sentences; one prisoner was serving five life sentences.

Another prisoner in the Block was Big Harry McKenney, who was alleged to have chopped up three men, and a young boy. I always had my doubts about Big Harry; the evidence against him was a bit flimsy.

I had spoken to Big Harry on many occasions and whilst being a villain and major crook he did not come over as someone who could kill. Every time he sent off an appeal, he never received one reply during my eighteen months working in the Special Security Block.

Others prisoners included four IRA prisoners, who had been found guilty of mass murder. I shall not name them because they are now free men, following the 'Good Friday Agreement'.

Whilst I had sympathy in their cause, I could never condone the way they murdered in an attempt to further it. The way they went about it disgusted me to the core. Soldiers of any nation that kill indiscriminately should be shot if found guilty. That also goes for those involved in the Bloody Sunday massacre.

Black Panther Neilson would elect to stay in his cell for most of the time. However, he was free to go anywhere inside or outside of the unit. Neilson would spend an hour every day marching like a regimental sergeant major on the exercise yard. Sometimes, he might spend an hour on his vegetable plot. Did I write vegetable plot? Yes! It was not a misprint.

These dozen or so prisoners had everything to make their very long and very secure sentences as comfortable as possible. After all, it is only the taxpayers' money, and it appeared to me that it was a case of peace at any price.

Neilson would spend most of the day and night painting in oils. I can only describe his paintings as the work of a genius. One day I am sure his paintings will be well sought after. Not just because it was the Black Panther that painted them, but because of his skill in his chosen art. He is a very gifted person. What a waste for God to give such an evil animal like Neilson such a talent. He was a loner and mixed with no other prisoners. He was allocated a period to use the video and would always watch nature and animal programmes. The TV images became the subjects of his paintings. He gave the staff no problems and I feel that he had accepted that he would never be released. A decision supported by everyone in the country.

All prisoners were unlocked and free to wander anywhere within the unit. Maximum security meant just that. Three other prisoners I will always remember were all members of the IRA and guilty of many atrocious crimes, I must state quite categorically that I did believe in their cause, but I could never condone the calculated killings which they carried out.

Carried out in such a barbaric manner, thinking they could change the political shape of Northern Ireland. All three prisoners were dedicated to their cause. They saw themselves as soldiers. They acted like military personnel and they considered themselves political martyrs. Their daily routines could be timed to the minute. They all used every facility in the unit to keep their bodies and minds sound. All were good at art and woodwork and they were all good athletes. It is a fact that if you could forget the horrific crimes they had committed, they came over as very nice young men. For most of the time they kept themselves to themselves and only spoke to staff when they had to.

When they came into my office they would hand to me their requests and applications to me on a piece of notepaper. We would only speak if there appeared to be a query. They were doing the time so how they did it was up to them. I did not care one way or the other.

One day an officer had placed one of the IRA prisoners on Governor's report, for a breach of the rules. A very rare event, but that is how upper management would always want it (peace at nearly any price). When the prisoners went out on to the exercise yard, they had to go through double doors, via a very small recess. These doors had to be unlocked by staff in the ECR. (To give more details would not be in the interests of security.)

I had noticed in the location log that all three IRA prisoners were out on the yard together. This was a very rare occurrence. I had noticed that only Neilson was inside the unit. All six other prisoners were on the yard. A dog handler was assisting on the yard, I asked Officer Ashgrove to take over from me in the office. I wanted to have a snoop around the unit whilst it was quiet.

It was pure chance that Officer Ashgrove and I had changed places. This officer had placed one of the IRA prisoners on Governor's report earlier in the day. The three crafty IRA prisoners had worked out just which officer was inside the unit. They saw this as a chance to have a go at Officer Ashgrove. They had expected Officer Ashgrove to receive them when they entered the unit via the double doors. When the officer entered the unit with an IRA prisoner, he was handed over to me. The prisoner looked disappointed and shocked to see me standing there, he said nothing, but he looked dejected.

Another IRA prisoner was let into the unit. (An officer from the yard should have returned into the unit and stayed in the unit.) As the officer left to go back to the yard, I told the officer not to allow any more prisoners back until we had an officer from the yard to increase staff inside the unit.

As soon as the officer returned to the yard, all hell broke loose. Both IRA prisoners picked up snooker cues (yes they had a small snooker table) and thrust it into the green beige tearing it to threads.

One of them shouted, "Where's that bastard Ashgrove?"

He wielded the cue smashing everything he could hit.

Officer Ashgrove had already rung the alarm bell, so I knew twenty or more staff would be on the scene within minutes. One prisoner threw the TV set at me, it missed, and I then moved in on him and secured him in a bear hug.

An old screw I may be, but I weighed seventeen stones, so he was going nowhere, doing nothing.

One prisoner was venting his anger out on the furniture and video recorders. He even pulled all the flower-patterned curtains down. (Yes! Curtains)

Officer Ashgrove had left the office to assist me and had overpowered one of the rioters; using the training he had received to cover such an incident. Unknown to the rioters Senior Officer Bull had called into the unit to get a prisoner's signature for cash handed in on a visit. He took charge of the telephones and other office communications.

The next thing I remember was twenty or more staff grabbing the prisoners and whisking them off to their cells. The exercise yard was cleared and all prisoners were locked in their cells. The place was a wreck; I had to have a fag and a sit down. The whole incident had probably lasted less than five minutes but I was that shattered, it felt as if it had lasted for hours.

Both prisoners were charged and placed before the Governor. What can you sentence a prisoner to who is serving several life sentences? During all adjudications IRA prisoners stroll in, slouch and never reply to any question put to them. A bloody farce to say the least, but that is the system, what have things come to? Several days later, a new TV, new video, and new curtains were brought into the unit. Prisoners were back mixing freely with the others, what a carry on! An excerpt from a 'Carry On' film, perhaps!

One day in October 1993, I went on duty as usual, I was on the afternoon shift. I took over from the Senior Officer who was finishing his shift. He said to me, "We received David Martin yesterday; he's going to be a handful."

Every one knew who David Martin was. Branded by the press as the 'the most wanted man in Britain', he had received a twenty-five year sentence, for firearms and other offences. He was the subject of the 'Waldorf shooting'.

When Martin's girlfriend, Sue Stephens, was travelling in a taxi with Waldorf, the police shot Waldorf thinking it was David Martin. Waldorf very nearly lost his life and later sued the police and was awarded very substantial damages. Martin remained at large for some time, causing a great deal of embarrassment to the police and to the Government.

At last, they caught their man, and the sentence of twenty-five years for such offences reflected just how much embarrassment he had caused them.

It was a policy of mine to have a talk with every new prisoner who arrived in the unit. It gave some insight into the prisoner's mood and his attitude at that time.

When I saw Martin I was shocked at the resemblance he had to my eldest son, also called David. I asked Martin what his attitude was to such a long prison sentence. He shrugged his shoulders and said, "I was not sentenced for the crimes but for the publicity and the bloody run-around I gave the Old Bill."

I had to agree, but did not tell him so. I told him that his cell would never be locked during the daytime and I told him of the many excellent facilities we had in the unit - snooker, table tennis, a gym, TV, video, and a large exercise yard with gardening plots and an area for tennis or five-a-side football. All designed to help him to pass the time.

Various tutors came into the unit to teach art, woodwork and physical training. I told him that it would be to his advantage to take part and however long his sentence appeared now, things can change and experience had taught me that an active mind is a healthy mind. I also told him that if he had any problems at all, to inform any member of staff. If we could help, we would.

He said, "Thanks for the lecture, but I do not intend staying here long."

At that time I thought he was thinking of escape. Escape from the SSB at Parkhurst was not possible and I say that with 100 percent certainty. I now know that he was thinking of a more morbid form of escape.

Over the next month or so, Martin became friendly with 'Big Harry' McKenney, (the alleged contract killer and the alleged murderer of a father and son).

He even got talking to Neilson (the Black Panther), which in itself was a major achievement. McKenney and Martin had two things in common. Both were appealing against conviction and sentence, and in my humble opinion, both had been given sentences that were well over the top.

I also came to believe later that the police had framed 'Big H' McKenney. It is now common knowledge that in the late 1960s to mid-1970s the Metropolitan Police had framed many gangland members for crimes they had not committed.

The Government needed to satisfy the press and the public. They wanted the gangs off the streets at any price. The general Election was just around the corner. The Government wanted to show the people just who was in charge.

Martin and 'Big H' appeared to be getting on well together. I think 'Big H' had adopted young Martin. They would spend hours working on their appeals and in general conversation. Every now and then one of them would pop into my office and ask how to spell a certain word; I became so fed up with them disturbing me that I lent them a dictionary.

I thought both were wasting their time with their appeals, especially in the present political climate, but it kept the peace and they appeared content.

Just before Christmas, I noticed a change in Martin's behaviour. He had become very unhappy and depressed.

I reported these changes to the Governor at the 'Heads of Departments' meeting. The Medical Officer took note, and the medical staff then saw Martin on a regular basis; medication was prescribed.

In the evenings Martin was never out of my office, asking for extra letters to write to his girlfriend, Sue.

An extra letter was referred to as a 'special letter', or a 'canteen letter', which had to be paid for by the prisoner. These were issued at the discretion of the Governor. The senior officers represented the Governor so we could be more generous than we would be on a normal wing. However there was a limit; every letter had to be recorded on the prisoner's letter sheet. This was retained in the security department and every time I issued a special letter, I had to inform our security. The Security Principal Officer reprimanded me for issuing too many letters.

I informed Martin that from now on all extra letters would have to be sanctioned by the Governor himself; the Governor was more than understanding, so nothing had actually changed.

I had also noticed that Martin could not keep still. He had to be on the move all of the time; he was just like a bear with a sore arse.

Every evening he would ask me if letters had arrived from Sue. I told him that I could only give him letters that we had received. He was very depressed. He would become very agitated and sometimes aggressive, not towards me, but with himself. It was at this time that I now suspected that he was planning something.

I knew that escape was impossible. Nevertheless all staff in the unit was once again reminded to keep a special eye on Martin; even 'Big H' had suggested to me that Martin was cracking up.

'Big H' stopped associating with Martin. Martin became a very miserable, unhappy and lonely young man. A Christmas parcel had arrived from his parents. Martin came into the office, threw the contents on my desk and said, "Send the fucking things back; I don't want anything from them."

I tried to make him see sense, but he seemed to be on another planet. He now spent most of the day alone, reading the few letters he had received from Sue, over and over again.

He would not speak to me now. I did my utmost to try to get him to snap out of his depression. He then started to spend most of the time in his cell. All unit staff was

informed of this prisoner's mood change. On reflection, I do feel that Martin should have been located into the prison hospital at this time.

Martin was a category 'A' prisoner, but such a high security risk could not be catered for, even in our very secure hospital wing. However, those at Head Office who make such decisions would never agree to Martin leaving the SSB. No more letters were received from Sue. His depression deepened and I knew that things were becoming very serious. Staff was again notified regarding Martin's demise. 'Big H' told me one evening that Martin was not eating. Martin had started his hunger strike which was to last for nine days.

The medical staff was visiting him every two to three hours, all of them trying their best to encourage Martin to start eating again. It was sad to see Martin looking ill and drawn, even after only just over a week without food. He was drinking, but the vitamins that the hospital staff had slipped into the water were soon detected by Martin and were rejected.

In all my service, I have never seen a prisoner receive so much attention; however, Martin was special, not just because he was a notorious criminal, made so by the press and media. He was the subject of legal and political wrangling in the Houses of Parliament. He had become big news in the tabloids. The prison's Public Relations Officer's telephone never stopped ringing. He in turn would then contact the Assistant Governor, responsible for Martin's press releases. The office telephones never stopped ringing.

David Martin gave up his hunger strike. It appeared that he had come out of his depression and gradually started mixing with 'Big H' and speaking to Neilson. Martin had put an end to his hunger strike because he was feeling very sick and had been informed by the hospital staff that they were getting ready to force-feed him.

He had lost a great deal of weight. In the New Year, Martin's behaviour continued to be unstable, he again became very moody. His behaviour again started to cause the staff some concern. Sue had stopped writing to Martin altogether.

The medical staff did everything in their power to try to help Martin.

He would listen and talk to no one now. He would just sit on his bed looking into space. I tried many times to make conversation but it was like talking to a brick wall. Not even 'Big H' could get through to him.

Martin was a very sick man, mentally and physically.

He should have been in the hospital; I have already given the reason why he would not be allowed in the prison hospital. He was a category 'A' prisoner and a very great risk. I informed all staff to keep an extra special eye on him.

On Sunday, 11 March 1984 I was sitting in my office when I heard a commotion coming from the direction of the association, TV and video room. I went to investigate. Neilson and Martin were squaring up to each other, there were a few shoves and pushes, but no blows were struck.

'Big H' was sitting in the corner of the room reading a book; he never let the incident take his eyes off his book.

I placed myself between the two of them and told them to stop 'pissing about'.

I asked what the argument was all about. Martin told me it was his turn to use the video. I checked the roster on the wall and it clearly indicated that it was Neilson's turn. I explained this fact to Martin but he then adopted an aggressive attitude towards me and pushed me in the chest. It was not a hard push and weighing seventeen stones, it would require a harder push than that to even budge me.

I told both prisoners that if they could not abide by the rules without arguing with each other, I would have no alternative but to remove the video from the unit. Other staff had now arrived and 'Big H' came over and told Martin that he was in the wrong.

'Big H' said, "Grow up Martin and act your bloody age."

Martin then became very aggressive, throwing punches and swearing. Thankfully, none of his punches came into contact with anyone.

Martin grabbed 'Big H' around the waist and shouted hysterically, "I will take the bloody lot of you on, you're all bloody bastards."

Considering the massive size of 'Big H' and the number of staff now present, Martin was in a no win, no go anywhere situation. 'Big H' again told Martin to grow up and stop acting like a little boy. By this time Martin was weeping profusely, swearing, and kicking out. I ordered staff to locate Martin in his cell and to lock the door.

A very rare occurrence in this unit, but I thought that the locking of Martin's cell door was in Martin's best interest; at that time I was convinced that Martin was a very sick man. I placed Martin on 'special watch'. (Special watch means that a prisoner is seen and observed every 15 minutes and everything that is observed is recorded in a book). The Governor, Medical Officer and all staff were informed of my decision.

After about an hour I visited Martin in his cell, he was still sobbing, but said nothing. I told him that I was going to leave his cell door open and that he could come and go as he pleased. I told him that the sooner he got back mixing with the others, the sooner the incident would be forgotten. I told him that 'Big H' had asked about him. He sat up, and said to me, "Piss off! Piss off!"

I left and left his door open. All staff was informed that on no account must any tool of any description be issued until further notice. The woodwork and art rooms were locked. I telephoned the Medical Officer and requested that he should visit Martin as soon as possible.

He arrived about ten minutes later. The Medical Officer spent twenty –twenty-five minutes with Martin. As the medical officer left the unit he said to me, "He has refused all medication."

I went to see Martin again. He was calling for Sue, his girlfriend. Martin was suffering from a broken heart.

I visited Martin many times to try to encourage him to get back into his normal routines. He was not in the slightest interested; he was in a world of his own.

I last saw David Martin at about five o'clock on 13 March 1984. I went to his cell; Martin was sat on his bed weeping. I said, "I am going off duty so let us hope that you are in a better mood tomorrow."

Martin looked up, tears streaming down his cheeks, and said, "Fuck off you old cunt."

I did not reply.

On the evening of 13 March 1984 my wife and I were celebrating 32 years of wedded bliss, two days early, because most of the family could not make it on the fifteenth. We held the celebration at our home with family and friends; as usual, we were having plenty to eat and drink.

My enjoyment came to a sudden end when a newsflash came up on the TV. David Martin had hanged himself in his cell at Parkhurst Prison. Although shocked, I was not surprised. David Martin had already decided to take his own life at the time Susan had stopped communicating with him. No letters and no visits from Sue were far too much for Martin to handle. How had he taken his own life, in spite of having been observed at fifteen minute intervals?

His cell door was not locked; normal activity was going on, as was the case at that time in the evening. I just could not understand how it had been allowed to happen.

I was upset; Martin was a criminal and had been in a great deal of trouble, but to end his young life in this way was way off the mark.

I went on duty the next day. Martin's body had been removed to the mortuary at St Mary's hospital, just across the road from the prison. The unit's routine carried on as normal. The telephone rang more than usual. A press officer (Governor Grade) dealt with all enquiries.

All logbooks (daily diaries) were taken away for scrutiny. The police liaison officer interviewed all staff who had worked in the unit, statements were taken.

This is just routine practice in this type of case; enquiries have to be made if only to try to find a scapegoat.

It had been established that Martin had used a short length of electric cable that he had cut from the communal washing machine to hang himself with. On the officers' next visit to check Martin, they found him hanging from the bars of his cell window. He was still warm and there was slight movement of the legs and arms. Officers Dean and Austin cut Martin free and they tried desperately to resuscitate him. Hospital staff arrived within minutes, but there was nothing that could be done. Martin was dead.

The Medical Officer had arrived and had officially pronounced Martin dead. Martin once told me he would never complete his sentence, it need not have ended in this way. I am sure that his sentence would have been reduced on appeal. No scapegoats had been found. It was suggested the washing machine cable should have been shorter, a case of being wise after the event. Why have washing machines in the unit in the first place?

Once someone has decided to take their own life, apart from chaining them to a wall 24 hours a day, it is virtually impossible to stop them. With all the tools and knives in the unit we were lucky that he did not decide to take a few others with him. That fact alone tells me he was not evil.

The custodial sentence that Martin had received was far too harsh. He had not committed rape or murder. He had paid the price because of a police blunder and the rejection of the girl he loved very much. The media must take some blame; they hounded Susan to such an extent that her parents gradually persuaded her to forget him. One of the last things Martin ever said to me was,

"I love Sue and always will and if you see my mother tell her I'm sorry and thank her for the chocolates."

I never did tell Mrs Martin, because we were not allowed to discuss the issue with anyone (Official Secrets Act).

How times have changed, Lord Archer and Claire Short have spilled the beans, and even ex-cabinet minister Claire Short says just about anything she wants to. Did they never sign the Official Secrets Act? It all depends who you are and what damage could be caused if the Government did decide to prosecute. Far too much would come out into the public domain if issues like this went to court. Like everything else, one rule for them, and other rules for us.

I was very hurt by Martin's death. I do feel that, on reflection, I could not have done any more to prevent this tragedy. In hindsight, Martin should have been located in the prison hospital, but the fear that he might escape deterred the Home Office from making what would have been the right decision.

At the Coroner's Inquest, a letter that Martin had left was produced. It was not read out to the Court, but shown to the members of the Bench only. The Coroner recorded a verdict of 'suicide'. The National Press had a field day, as they usually do, blowing everything out of all proportion.

Every prisoner who was located in the Special Security Block was named, yet only Neilson and 'Big H' had played any role in the lead up to Martin's death, and a minor role at that. So much for security, who then leaked the names to the press? The details came from somewhere and I would wager that the informant did not wear a uniform or cap. Let us be honest. David Martin was a minor crook who had just thought that the time was ripe to move up into the big-time.

As I have already stated, an appeal against his long sentence would, I feel, have been upheld and his sentence reduced. Martin could not wait for this to happen; in spite of all the advice he had been given. Martin once said to me, "Mr Smith I can see no light at the end of the tunnel, what is the point of it all?"

David Martin was not an evil monster like most of them in the Special Security Block.

All the newspaper talk about Martin being a cross-dresser and a transvestite was a figment of the newspaper reporters' imagination. He did dress as a woman, but only to disguise himself to escape police detection. Martin was travelling in another taxi behind the taxi that Sue and Waldorf were in; he was dressed as a woman on the night to avoid detection. Waldorf was shot.

'Big H' appeared to be getting on well with the other prisoners; he was much older and more mature. Big Harry McKenney was about the same age as I was; he was well over six feet tall, taller than I was, but as I was putting on weight; big 'H' was losing it. I had first met 'Big H' when he was first sentenced some eight years previously. Then he was built like a brick shithouse, yet was always the gentle giant. He did however have a tendency of being drawn into other prisoners' problems.

He used to call into my office to have a chat, often saying, "Those little boys wind me up."

'Big H' was the unit's barber. Yes! We did have haircutting tools, scissors included. He would never cut the hair of the IRA prisoners; he called them scum, but would give the rest of the prisoners a trim.

I was going to my mate's Silver Wedding party in a couple of day's time; I had not been to the barbers for months, all the overtime that I was working. I was sat in the office with a couple of staff; 'Big H' was sitting in the corner reading the newspaper. I just happened to say that I needed a hair cut to go to a party. Big 'H' said to me, "I'll give your hair a trim if you want, Mr Smith."

I thought for a while, and agreed. 'Big H' got to work. One of the staff said the Chief and Governor were on their way in to the unit. I said, "So what, this is the only chance I've had to have a hair cut."

The Governor and Chief walked into my office. 'Big H' carried on cutting my hair. I said, "All is quiet and correct sir, all seven category 'A's are inside the unit, there are none on the exercise yard."

Both the Chief and the Governor gave me a look of astonishment. The Governor signed the visitor's book, had another look at the barber, and departed. One officer said to me that he did not think they had thought it a good idea, 'Big H' cutting my hair.

Twenty or so minutes later the telephone rang. It was the Chief Officer's clerk, he said, "Senior Officer Smith sir, the Chief Officer wants you to call into his office when you go for lunch."

I said, "OK!"

On my way to lunch, I called into the Chief's office. He bawled, "What the hell are you doing letting that mad axe man cut your hair? The Governor was shocked, to say the least!"

I said, "Well, Chief I do not see it as a problem; they have hammers, chisels, knives, and mallets in the unit, not to mention the saws and screwdrivers. If they wanted to bump me off, they could do it any time, and would you please inform the Governor that it was he who allowed the hairdressing set and all those other tools into the unit. Anyway chief, 'Big H' would not have cut my throat; he had not received the quarter ounce of tobacco I had promised him."

The Chief said, "Sod off! You have a bloody answer for everything."

Eighteen months in the Special Security block was long enough for anyone; also, it was a policy of management to move staff around so as not to allow any member of staff to become too familiar with the prisoners. I had enjoyed my work in the block and had shared the responsibility with a nice chap by the name of Alex Thearle. He was about the same age as me but more of an introvert, not a bit like me. Maybe he had more sense. I had completed well over my twelve-month stint, so someone must have been satisfied.

My next posting was to be in joint charge of the Reception Unit. Two senior officers covered this post, working shifts to cover the 24 hour day (having written that, we usually worked an eight hour shift), working a double shift to cover for one of us being on leave, holidays or sickness.

The Senior Officer already in Reception was Harry Hampson.

He was a Scot who thought he was God's gift to the service. He loved to tell me how good he was at the job, but not as keen to show me how to do things.

Fortunately, we had an orderly who had worked in Reception for nearly five years. His name was Mac. He was a short, stocky man, as wide as he was tall and very strong. He kept himself in good shape by using his home-made weights, which he kept in the back of the property store. He knew the reception and discharge routine better than anyone did. He knew every prisoner's personal property box number and knew exactly just what was inside, down to a pair of socks.

He was an official Rule 43 and his cell was located on the punishment wing, which was the next building. Being a Rule 43 he could not associate with other prisoners because he had been found guilty of rape and of stabbing a man. He had received ten years detention, which carries no remission for good behaviour. Mac was found guilty of raping the owner of a hotel where he worked as a barman.

The week before, he had slept with the hotel owner and she had agreed to have intercourse; the following week she cried rape. On hearing her cries for help, the night watchman came to assist and Mac stabbed the man with some scissors. The owner of the hotel and Mac had both drank far too much alcohol. Mac had accepted his sentence and never put a foot out of place; he was the most trustworthy and loyal orderly I had ever known. Very hard-working and besides working very long hours in reception, he also cleaned the punishment blocks, officers' canteen and rest room.

He knew Reception better than the back of his hand. There were about 400 prisoners and Mac knew everything about all of them, he was a human index file. He showed me the routines and all I had to know and I was soon on a par with super screw Harry.

Receptions could arrive at any time of day or night but the main reception and transfer day was Wednesday.

Receptions came mainly from the London prisons and from remand centres. Transfers would be going back to the same prisons, with the same escorts. We had around four to six prisoners going on release every week, depending on their discharge date. When a prisoner reaches his discharge date he must be released, otherwise the Governor would be in serious trouble.

This was the start of the most enjoyable job since I left the farm at Aylesbury all those years earlier. The family loved the Isle of Wight, so much so that my eldest daughter Donna and her family, sold their house in Aylesbury, and came to live quite close to us.

Harry, the other senior officer, used to double up with me on a Wednesday, if we had a lot of receptions and transfers. This is the only time we would work together. On other days we would leave notes on a pad on what had to be done. The notes on the pad were just a formality because our orderly, Mac, would be fully aware of what was going on. To be honest he could have run reception on his own; he was a very loyal and honest person. It is a fact that the hotel manager had shouted rape, but many times before she had willingly consented to sex with Mac. The stabbing of the waiter could not be condoned.

I had noticed that when prisoners arrived from London most of them knew me. They saw Parkhurst as an escape from the harsh routines of Wandsworth, they were right. Parkhurst had a regime not unlike a Butlin's holiday camp. I told Mac that when I was on duty all receptions would be respectful towards the staff and I would not tolerate foul language. Reception, when I was on duty would be just like an extension of HMP Wandsworth.

Mac said, "Christ! Talk about chalk and cheese. You are the boss Mr Smith, but how Harry is going to take to the rule I do not know!"

I replied, "What standards Harry adopts do not affect me. When Harry is in charge, he is in charge; he must work to his own standards."

To be honest, Harry, although being a typical Parkhurst officer, was a disciplinarian at heart, having served in the army before joining the prison service. The fact that I had longer service in my rank did mean I was more senior to Harry.

I remember on one occasion a reception from London told me to 'fuck off' when I told him told to get a move on, Mac jumped over the counter, pinned him against the wall and said, "Do not talk to my boss like that or I'll break your back."

The new arrival cowered away and moved into the holding area. Mac was a very useful man to have on your side. Everyone entering or leaving Reception was searched for prohibited items, such as drugs or handmade knives, but as they had gone through the same procedure when leaving their last establishment, very little was ever found.

At Parkhurst, prisoners were allowed to have far more extra items in their possession, including record players and records, some civilian sports gear, trainers, and sets of games etc. Every item had to be recorded on the prisoners' property card. Valuables would be locked in the cashier's safe until discharge. All items being sent out by post or handed out on a visit had to be checked by Reception staff before leaving the establishment.

Nothing ever got past us, Mac saw to that.

Neilson, the 'Black Panther', had started sending his paintings out to his family. These paintings were of a very high standard. He was allowed to send six out every month, but the Governor had ordered that Neilson must not sign his work. When the first paintings arrived into Reception, Mac said he would give the paintings the once over, before packing ready for posting. He went into his little room in the box stores.

Mac said, "I thought the Governor had said that Neilson had not to sign his paintings? The crafty sod has signed every one of them."

Mac showed me how; in each bottom right-hand corner he had placed his signature on top of the oil paint, and then used watercolours to cover his signature.

Neilson was reported to the Governor. It was pointless nicking (placing a prisoner on a Governor's report) a prisoner who was serving several life sentences, and who had not a cat in hell's chance of ever being given his freedom. The Governor ordered that no paintings were to be sent out for two years. When the public and experts see those paintings it will not matter who painted them, believe me, they are masterpieces.

Harry had left for 'B' wing and Robby replaced him. Robby was a young Senior Officer who had just gained promotion; he was a breath of fresh air. I had sons older than he was. He was a very bright young man (obviously not an ex-service man), quiet and reserved. It was not long before he had learned the basics of the job.

With Mac the orderly behind you, it was hard to make a mistake.

I had been working with Mac for about nine months. I never forgot he was a prisoner but we had a great working relationship. Although he may say he did all the work, I would not argue with that. We had many a laugh and a joke and Robby was quick to join in with us.

One day there were several officers in Reception and I said to them that no one could beat my orderly Mac in an arm wrestle. Everyone wanted to take up the challenge. One by one, Mac defeated them all. I called them a load of softies. I boasted.

"I can beat Mac, who will back against me?"

All of them said I could not win.

I said, "I will wager a pound each that I beat Mac, OK"

All agreed and Mac and I took up our positions.

I said, "Only one attempt, remember, I am a grandfather."

The contest began. Mac had short, stubby arms but they were bigger than my thighs. We heaved and panted. After about fifteen minutes, I finally got Mac's hand to the counter top.

I said to them, "There you are! It takes a bloody old man to show you the way."

All of them paid up and they left reception with their tails between their legs.

I said to Mac, "Well done, I think we made it look real. I will get you that quarter of an ounce of tobacco later."

Mac and I had set them up. No way could I have won that contest fairly; as I said earlier, we did have many laughs.

Later in the week two prisoners called into reception. One of them asked if he could show his Paul Pender guitar to the other one. They had been polite, I was not doing anything at the time and I thought it to be a reasonable request. I asked Mack to bring it from the property room. Mack handed the guitar over.

Then without any warning, he hit the other prisoner over the head with the guitar, and then said, "Now pig, stop writing letters to my wife!"

Both prisoners were charged with causing disorderly conduct; there was never a dull moment in reception.

I made mention in an earlier chapter of Sinman, the international drug baron, who died of a heart attack whilst serving a thirty year sentence in the Special Security Block. Whilst working in reception I received a Form 35, (internal inter-departmental message,) from the Governor informing me that Mrs Sinman, his widow, was making the journey from Australia to the UK to collect her late husband's property. There were about five large suitcases, all packed to the brim, which were stored in the back of the Reception box store. Mac our orderly knew exactly what was in the suitcases, down to the last silk tie.

All Sinman's jewellery and watches were stored in the cashier's office, which was situated in the main administration building.

Non-valuable items are recorded on the prisoner's property card in black ink, Sinman had about six cards. Most other prisoners had only one, a few had two.

Valuables were entered in red in the valuable column. If it was made of gold, it would be entered as Y/M (yellow metal) or if silver as W/M (white metal).

Sinman had no W/M on his card, everything was pure gold. However all gold items were always recorded as yellow metal, to avoid false claims. Anyway, we were not jewellery experts, watches and jewellery had to be listed in red and described as fully as possible. If the watch had a name, the name had to be entered.

Reception staff would only withdraw a prisoner's valuables the day before the prisoner was discharge, or prior to transfer to another prison.

The day of Mrs Sinman's visit drew ever closer. Mac had rigged up two large tables so that Mrs Sinman could inspect her late husband's property.

A few days before she was due I received a Form 35 which read, 'Mrs Sinman was not interested in her late husband's clothes or shoes et cetera.' She just wanted to collect his valuables and cash. It would appear that all of Mac's work had been in vain.

I telephoned the Governor and asked what I should do with the clothes et cetera. The Governor said,

"Take them all to a charity shop."

I asked Mac to pack all Sinman's gear up in boxes and I would take it to the charity shop when I had the time.

The next day Mac came into my office with the usual cup of tea, also a nice bacon sandwich. 'It must be my birthday,' I thought!

Mac said to me in a very quiet voice, "Mr Smith you know I am an honest person and I have worked very hard all these years for you and other senior officers."

This is not like Mac and I thought; this was not the Mac I had come to know. He usually comes straight out with things. What does he want?'

I said to Mac, "Right Mac, spit it out, what can I do for you?"

Mac said, "Well Mr Smith, Sinman was exactly the same size as me; even his crocodile shoes fit me. His suits he bought from France and all his silk shirts fit me. Can I swap them for mine?"

This request left me speechless, I paused a while then said, "I will have to give it some serious thought Mac."

Mac had loads of gear that had been given to him by prisoners going on discharge, whose gear did not fit them.

I thought about what Mac had asked me and I said to me, 'Well, it's only going to end up in a charity shop, and who knows whether the people that sort the clothes out cream off the best stuff for themselves?'

I called Mac into the office and said, "Yes! You can exchange the clothes et cetera, but only on a one-to-one basis; I do not want any alterations on the property card, OK!"

Mac replied, "Mr Smith, thank you."

Robby will have to be told, I want no secrets.

The exchange took place; I thought then and I still feel now that nothing dishonest was done - practical Christianity - just rewards for all Mac's loyal service.

We had started getting requests on Form 35s from the Wing Governor that Reg Kray wanted to check his property. Mac said we could only do it on a Saturday afternoon. I told the Wing Governor that it would be all right on a Saturday afternoon. Reginald Kray was soon knocking on the door of Reception. I opened the door, and said, "Who are you, and what do you want?"

I knew who he was and knew what he wanted; but I was playing hard to get; Mac was smiling in the background. Kray said, "I am Reg Kray, Mr Smith."

"Oh yes! You have come to check your gear. Go into the holding room and Mac will bring your boxes out."

(Just like Sinman, Kray had some very fine clothes and gear.)

Kray said to me, "I remember you from somewhere Mr Smith."

I replied, "You probably do, I've been inside longer than you."

Kray smiled and said, "I suppose you have but I've had enough. I think I last saw you at the Old Bailey at my trial and you once took me to see my brother Ronnie at Broadmoor."

Kray asked, "Do you mind if I try one of my suits on? Just to see if they still fit?"

I said, "That's OK! But I do not think they will fit you now. You appear to have shrunk a lot, or the clothes have expanded."

Kray said, "Old age and prison food."

Kray was about the same age as I was. Kray and I were in our mid-fifties.

He was not half the man he used to be. He reminded me of old man Steptoe; he even had the same accent. Kray came over as a very polite, cheerful and courteous man, but I knew that beneath that façade was a very cunning, devious and wicked criminal.

Whilst in prison Kray had never been in much trouble. However, we all knew he pulled the strings, inside and outside of the prison. He had some very powerful friends. Not all from them from the criminal fraternity, many came to visit him from the world of entertainment.

If there was trouble or any riot you could wager that Kray was somehow involved. Just like his gangland days, he got others to do his dirty work.

Kray started to visit Reception nearly every chance he got and his visits to Reception on Saturdays became a regular occurrence; approved, I must add, by a very sympathetic Wing Governor. Once a category 'A' prisoner, Kray was now Category 'B' which did mean he needed less supervision.

Those in high office thought it right to downgrade him, a decision I did agree with, after all he was nearing the end of a very long sentence.

Kray had made a friend of a young man I shall call Peter. Peter was in his mid-twenties and was a minor villain. They were inseparable; many thought they were having a gay relationship. On their joint visits to reception and the times, I saw them together when I was later transferred to 'B' wing; I saw absolutely no evidence to substantiate this rumour. I am sure that Kray just found younger company more to his taste and he treated Peter just like a son.

I do know Kray had private cash sent in for Peter and it went towards the purchase of a lovely expensive guitar.

I played guitar myself a little so when Kray and Peter found out about this, more visits to Reception were requested.

I did help Peter to put a few chords together. Kray said to Peter on one occasion, "When you're famous Peter you can tell everyone that Mr Smith helped you to start".

Mac and I had to have a little chuckle.

Over the next few months Kray would tell Peter, on his visits to Reception, all about his wicked deeds of the past and many were overheard.

I honestly believe that Reg Kray was trying to convince Peter that crime actually paid; such a happy, highflying life. What advice from a silly old gangster who had spent most of his life behind bars and whose dastardly behaviour had driven his young wife to suicide.

My tour of duty in Reception had come to an end. I had enjoyed the work, but I knew that all good things had to come to an end at some stage. It was going to be back to basics from now on. My next job was to be on Bravo Wing, 'B' wing for short.

'B' wing was about the worst place any prison officer could work. I am almost sure that management sent staff for a spell on this wing as a punishment. Most of the wing staff had only served at Parkhurst and had never seen how a real prison functioned; they just accepted their lot.

There was more discipline at one of the Butlin's holiday camps. The prisoners appeared to run the wing.

One evening whilst patrolling a landing, yes! I did patrol the landings, and not just to check out on the prisoners, you needed to keep an eye on some of the staff. I opened a cell and found two prisoners drinking hooch (home-made alcoholic drink). I went back down to the office and said to my second in command, "They have some hooch on number three landing, and we will go up and take them to the punishment wing."

My number two said, "That's just a waste of time, it will only upset everyone, and they will lock up nice and quiet at lock-up time."

This attitude was getting through to me. I could not accept this sloppy approach to prison discipline. It made the job both more difficult for the staff and more un-organised for the prisoners. Everyone benefits from good order and discipline.

At locking up time, I ordered the three officers to accompany me to the cell where I had seen the two prisoners drinking hooch. I opened the cell door, and one of them was pissed out of his mind.

I said to the officers, "Take him down to the punishment wing, he's nicked."

One officer said, "Have you seen the time sir?"

'Typical Parkhurst attitude,' I thought.

I said, "Down he goes, sod the time, this is a bloody prison, or…?"

Next day the prisoner appeared before the Governor and he lost seven days remission.

I know I had now become very unpopular with the staff, but you cannot run a prison in an undisciplined, unorganised fashion. Rules are rules, everyone should stick to them. These Parkhurst staff, (having never worked anywhere else) knew no better. They thought it better and easier to do the job in their shabby way; bad habits are very hard to break.

I had to have a talk to the Chief Officer. I told him that 'B' wing was a shambles. The lack of basic discipline and implementation of prison rules was getting me down.

The Chief said, 'Well Mr Smith I understand just how you feel, but Parkhurst is not going to change just for you, you were told to forget about Aylesbury and Wandsworth when you arrived here. If you cannot, then you have two options, put up with it or go through the gates."

What a bloody attitude to take, I thought. Perhaps! It is a good piece of advice after all. I am fifty-six now and another year will give me twenty-five years service. I will hang in for another year. Therefore, if you cannot beat them, join them. It did hurt me to admit to taking this easy way out.

My wife Jean had noticed a change in me. I was drinking more and for the first time in my life, I had become moody and restless. I seemed to be losing my temper at the slightest thing; the relationship with my wife was not what it should have been, she knew that there was something not right at my work. For the first time in my life, I was bringing my troubles home.

I went to see my doctor because I was drinking far too much. I was drinking in the hope that I would sleep better and get away from constantly thinking about the chaos in the prison. Chaos which only I appeared to be concerned about; chaos that I knew I could do nothing about.

My GP prescribed some antidepressant pills; that was the start of my mental demise.

The most dangerous times in any prison are when the majority of prisoners are out of their cells mixing at a time when staff cover is at its minimum; this would include association times and mealtimes.

Association time is for playing recreational games, such as table tennis, cards and snooker. This type of association would apply for all prisoners on 'B' wing; including category 'A' prisoners. I do believe that in today's prisons each prisoner has a personal TV in their cell; this must make it easier for both staff and prisoners.

Mealtimes can also be a hazardous time. In the larger prisons, two to three hundred prisoners can be out of their cells at any one time, as they collect their meals.

All meals are collected from the main kitchen and served on individual wings. It is at these times when old scores can best be settled, and the barons use their heavy mobs to collect their outstanding debts for tobacco or drugs. It is also a dangerous time for staff; many an officer has been slashed across his face with the prisoner's steel meal tray.

I can remember one young officer receiving a facial wound that required sixteen stitches; thankfully, attacks on staff were rare, it was usually inmate against inmate or gang against gang. However, the staff can soon restore peace and order.

Thankfully, at the start of an incident, the officer standing by the alarm bell would press the bell and staff would arrive in great numbers. Most times things were soon returned back to normal.

It was common practice for prisoners to delay the staff from getting off duty on time by playing tricks at any time of the day. The best ploy was for the prisoners who served the food to conveniently run short of food, so that the officer in charge of the food had to take a couple of servers to the main kitchen to obtain more food, this was an accepted occurrence.

The cook had always saved extra food, knowing what to expect every mealtime. Why the staff put up with this, I do not know! Well! I do know the reason, why? They had lost their control from many years of 'peace at any cost'. Parkhurst staff would do anything for peace and quiet. They dare not rock the boat. It was inbred in them, they knew of nothing else.

What a contrast; it was so much more difficult than working at Wandsworth, doing your job was made so much more difficult by this lack of discipline here at Parkhurst.

At lunchtime one day, the prisoners had arranged their usual delay tactics and it had succeeded. The staff had been delayed for lunch by fifteen minutes. I thought to myself, let us try to change things'.

The same delay tactic was again caused at the teatime break. I said to myself, 'enough is enough'.

When the staff had returned from their afternoon break;

I informed them that I would delay unlocking by the same amount of time that they had delayed us. I could detect that not many of the staff were in favour of my plan.

Well, after all, this was revolutionary; this was Parkhurst not Wandsworth.

I did delay unlocking by fifteen minutes and in spite of the 140 or so prisoners banging on their cell doors, I stood my ground. After the fifteen minutes were up, I gave the order to unlock. Not one prisoner said a word to me as they passed my office on their way to the association rooms and the TV room.

'Had I got away with it?' I thought. 'It can be done.'

I slept like a log that night.

Next morning all the prisoners were unlocked at the normal time. I had made my point. Well! I thought I had. Two members of the East End gang stood outside the wing's Principal Officer's office door, I asked them, could I help them.

Not one of them replied to me, so I ignored them.

The Principal Officer arrived at about eight o'clock to take requests for the Governor's attention; referred to generally as Governor's applications, I could sense that all was not well. The two-gang leaders wanted to see the boss. They wanted to complain about being unlocked late the night before. They met with the Principal Officer and made their complaint.

The Principal Officer called into my office and told me that they had all asked to complain to the Governor.

I said, "Ah well! So be it, let's await the outcome."

Later that day the Governor called me to his office, the Chief was at his side.

The Governor said, "I can understand the logic behind your actions Senior Officer Smith, but on no account must the prisoners be delayed ever again."

I said to the Governor, "For years they have been deliberately delaying staff, I thought a bit of their own medicine might just make them conform sir."

The Governor replied, "Mr Smith you must forget, you are not at Wandsworth now, how many times must I remind you of this?"

I replied, "I could never forget that sir, nor could I ever make a comparison; but with respect sir, I shall just say this, if I was the Governor of this shit-hole I would be ashamed of myself."

The Governor said, "Mr Smith you have said far too much already, this prison is about containment, nothing else; please leave my office."

I said, "Just one last thing sir before I leave - what happens when you lose that containment?"

The Governor snarled, "Get out! Shut the door behind you."

However, the Chief Officer did give me a wink as I left the office. He knew I was right, but if they wanted a regime like a holiday camp, so be it. I thought to myself, 'That's my promotion up the spout. Ah well! It is not the end of the world. Thank God I am coming to the end of my service. Much more of this and I would go round the bend

altogether; how near the truth I was.

Just after I had retired from the service, three category 'A' prisoners did break the containment. The prison was downgraded to a category class 'B' prison, this meant that many staff lost their jobs and had to be transferred to other establishments, mostly on the mainland.

I knew the system would collapse one day. Without proper discipline and control, things will always end up pear-shaped in the end. Regular Parkhurst staff had only themselves to blame, it was nothing but sheer unadulterated neglect.

On another occasion a prisoner came into my office and told me that there was going to be a fight at lock-up time. This prisoner had in the past been a reliable source of information; he was not a grass, just a prisoner who wanted to serve his sentence with the minimum of fuss and to get home in one piece.

He told me that three Turkish prisoners were going to be beaten up when they returned to their cells from the

TV room. I thought that this could be a racist attack, plain and simple.

I positioned extra staff to cover this possible event.

I had already pre-warned Security, the Orderly Officer. It is the Orderly Officer who is in charge of the whole prison. I also informed the Emergency Control Room.

The prisoners started to leave the TV room and they filed past my office. I went onto the landing, looked up towards number two landing, and leaning on the rails I could see the East End gang, obviously in a position where they could get a good view of the action. These bastards were nothing but overgrown thugs, all far too fat or too old to play an active role themselves. Why should they risk injury and possible loss of remission?

All of a sudden all hell broke loose. Shouting and swearing, about forty prisoners were running up the stairs towards numbers three and four landings, I then pressed the alarm bell. The evening duty Principal Officer had already positioned himself, with six or seven extra staff, just outside the main entrance, so when the alarm was heard they entered the wing as quickly as possible. We were always short of staff on the evening shift and at weekends.

Led by Principal Officer Hampson they headed straight into the centre of the affray. Blows were being struck, and to me it appeared we had the makings of a major disturbance, or was this an organised disturbance, a decoy perhaps, for a mass escape?

I had to stay near the office to be able to communicate. I had a deep suspicion that this could be a set-up for a major breakout. I ordered an officer to take the padlock and chain from the TV corridor door and secure it on the main exit door; this action made the wing far more secure.

A couple of staff suggested that I should have gone into the thick of things. What purpose or difference would I have made? My main concern was the security of my wing. Had 140 prisoners got out of the wing and on to the yards, no one could have predicted the serious consequences that would have followed. We did not have the staff to cope with a mass escape.

Principal Officer Hampson with seven or eight staff quelled the disturbance and the prison was made secure. All received commendations for bravery, which were very well deserved.

I was, and remain positive, that the action I took was the right action, the disturbance was contained within the wing, and no one was seriously injured. When will those at the top realise that ten officers cannot control 140 rioting prisoners? They did on this occasion, but we may not be as lucky next time.

On 'B' wing we had all the scum of the jail; several should have been classified as being 'mental'. Many were violent and the presence of Reg Kray did not help matters. I am sure that all of the nutcases went out of their way to try to impress him and the East End gang by continually causing disruption.

This disruptive behaviour had not just started when I arrived on the wing, it had been going on for years, and was totally acceptable to the staff who had only worked at Parkhurst.

Two other officers and I, who had worked in other prisons, found it very unacceptable. This lack of discipline and the bending of the prison rules caused a great deal of unnecessary stress. I myself found solace in a glass or two of brandy when I got home; it was becoming a very bad habit and did not go unnoticed by my wife and young teenage son.

These long-term prisoners thrive on disruption and causing mayhem. It is ironic that these same prisoners would toe the line at any other prison; but this was Parkhurst where the ice cream van would be allowed access to the recreation areas at weekends, I do not jest.

They will do almost anything to rock the boat; it is all a big joke to them. It is all part of passing their time at whatever cost to other people.

Staff and prisoners alike sometimes get hurt in these skirmishes; I can remember one young officer receiving a back injury that forced him to be medically discharged. The last time I saw this officer he had been in a neck support for almost fifteen years.

Far too many staff had to take early medical retirement, caused by, stokes, heart attacks, alcoholism and mental breakdowns, all brought about by stress, alcohol, tobacco and far too many hours spent on duty. Those at the top fixed the retirement age at fifty-five years of age; they knew exactly what they were doing. You are then put out to grass. They do give you a moderate pension, but that alone will not pay the bills until you attain the age of sixty-five, when you then qualify for your Old Age Pension.

Whenever a disturbance was in full flight on the wing - a regular occurrence on 'B' wing - you could bet your bottom dollar that Reg Kray would be gazing down from his high vantage point on number three landing; always at his side was his sidekick, young Peter.

Every now and then a fight or an argument between prisoners would flare up, nothing very serious on most occasions, but just enough to disrupt the staff and the wing routines.

We had a dozen mental cases on the wing, which really should have been located in the prison hospital. However, at weekends to give the hospital staff a quieter time, they would conveniently locate these nutcases onto 'B' wing. The other prisoners seized upon this to wind them up to get them to cause as much disruption as possible.

One prisoner, who was serving a life sentence, would start to mop the floor just before the Governor came round on his daily inspection; nothing of great significance, but enough to allow the East End gang, who were located just above the office, an excuse to make jokes about his daily performance. Personally I would have had him locked in his cell before every Governor's visit. This prisoner was the wing comedian, but this sort of clowning about had been accepted on 'B' wing for years. It was not done for normal jollification, but just to cause disruption and embarrassment to the wing staff. It was far too late for me to change anything; if you cannot beat them, join them.

I hate keep repeating the latter, but it is so true.

I remember sitting in the wing office one day when an irate prisoner entered my office, without first knocking. Other staff was present. He started to rant and rage and I thought - this chap has a problem.

"What's your problem Kelly?"

I asked.

Kelly said, "Look at this! You call this a fucking dinner guv? I would not give it to a pig."

I said, "Well, there is nothing I can do at this time, dinner has been served and all the food has gone back to the main kitchen. You will have to make an official complaint to the Governor. I will make an entry in the food complaints book."

This book was examined weekly by the Governor and shown to the prison cook, who in fairness worked wonders with the prisoners' menu, considering the meagre allowance he was allowed for each prisoner.

The next thing I remember was having nearly the whole contents of the prisoner's meal thrown all over me. I was covered from head to foot with soup, cabbage and spuds, thankfully the pudding and custard missed me.

The prisoner was taken to the punishment wing and I charge him with assaulting an officer.

Next day Kelly appeared before the Governor. I gave out my evidence to the Governor; the clerk records all the evidence on a large white paper form.

The Governor said, "Well, Kelly! You have heard the officer's evidence, how do you plead?"

Kelly said, "Not guilty sir."

The Governor said, "Have you anything to say in mitigation Kelly?"

Kelly said, "Well sir, I get discharged next week and was getting over excited at the prospect of going home."

The Governor said, "Well Kelly, I have listened to the evidence and I find you guilty of the charge."

The Governor spoke in such a soft tone of voice, I thought he was going to burst out in tears.

The Governor said to Kelly, "You will miss your association and TV until your discharge."

I was flabbergasted! At any other prison, he would have lost at least twenty-eight days remission for such an offence. The prisoner was escorted from the room.

The Governor said, "Thank you Mr Smith, you may leave."

I was fuming. I said, "Governor Sir, a prisoner assaults an officer in sight of other members of staff and that is the only punishment you can dish out? What example and message does this send out to the other prisoners? One thing is certain sir; I shall never place another prisoner before you ever again. You have lost control. This prison is a bloody shambles. How do expect us to do our job without the proper back-up?"

The Chief Officer who had been present said to me, "You have had your say now leave. I will see you in my office at noon."

He had to say something, but deep down I knew he agreed with what I said. I should not have said what I did, I should have kept my thoughts to myself, but we all must speak our minds from time to time, or should we? I do feel we should. I did meet with the Chief at noon but all he said was, "Do try to control your personal feelings; after all, the Governor is the Governor."

So, be it! I thought as I left the Chief's office. I never did place a prisoner on a charge ever again. I had joined the ranks of 'B' wing staff. If you cannot beat them, join them. I have used that cliché somewhere before; but it is so very appropriate.

I felt that I had been humiliated; I was saddened that it had come to this. I knew that my time as a senior prison officer was nearing the end. The enthusiasm I once enjoyed for the job had gone. Also, the job itself was changing. No longer were we prison officers; just Butlin's Redcoats dressed in blue.

They say that Kray wrote his life story. A film

was made about his seedy past, he made him a fortune. Other convicts have prospered from their time spent in prisons. They have books written about their exploits; ninety-nine percent is made up bullshit. So, when you see a book written by an ex-convict on a bookshelf or even in a library take it from me - it is most likely pure fiction.

Hard Men? No! Jelly Babies.

Chapter 13
Enough is enough

One morning I set off to go on duty, I was feeling rotten; far too much whisky the night before. I thought to myself. Why do I do it? As I got closer and closer to the main prison gate, my body started to shake and tremble. I was just about to knock on the door to the prison when a very strange feeling came over me.

I turned and ran all the way home; on entering the house I said to my wife, "I just cannot go into the prison."

Jean said, "Sit down love; I will make you a nice cup of tea. I think you are sickening for something. Go to bed and I will bring the drink up to you."

I went to bed, and although it was summer, I was cold and shaking like a leaf. Jean entered the bedroom; she sensed something was not right.

Jean said to me.

"I am getting the doctor to visit you."

I did not reply, because I also knew that something was amiss.

The doctor arrived, Doctor Hooper, I had known him a long time, so I knew that I had to be straight with him.

He gave me a full examination and said, "Well, Mr Smith I can find nothing physically wrong with you, your blood pressure is a little on the high side, but apart from that I can find nothing wrong."

I then started to shake again. I told the doctor just what had happened earlier that morning.

The doctor said, "You have been overdoing things at that prison, I see far too many prison staff that show the same symptoms as you are showing. I call it the Prison Officers' Syndrome.

I will prescribe some medication for you to help calm you down. Take a week off duty and come and see me in a week's time."

Jean said, "It is obvious to me that you have been in that job far too long, you are not as young as you used to be, Duncan and I have noticed the change in you, and you should leave that whisky alone, it will kill you."

I went off to sleep. I went to see my GP a week later and he asked how I was. I said, "Doctor I am just too scared to go to work. Every time I think about returning, I become more scared."

The doctor said, "Do not worry it has happened to many people in occupations where there is a high stress factor. Occupational stress takes certain chemicals out of our systems, what we have to do are to try to replace them.

We will keep you on the same medication, but you're not fit for duty yet; it could take a long time."

How right he was, it was the beginning of the most miserable time of my life. Not being on duty for such a long period, I soon became bored and it was obvious that I was getting on Jean's nerves; I appeared to have lost all interest in life.

I could not take a drink; that was taboo. The medication was not compatible with the alcohol.

After a couple of weeks I went to the doctor to inform him that I wanted to go back on duty. To be honest, I did not want to go back on duty, I was just bored and fast becoming ashamed of myself; I had to get off my arse and make an effort. The doctor thought that I was rushing things, but reluctantly, he signed me fit for duty.

I telephoned the Chief Officer to inform him that I was returning to duty; he sounded pleased and said that I should pop in to see him before going to my office.

I set off to the prison feeling rather proud of myself; after all, I was only doing something I had done for 25 years. As I approached the prison my body started to tremble, I just had to make the effort. Looking back to that time, I can only describe it as a feeling of fear and uncertainty. Fear of what, I do not know?

I knocked on the prison gate. The officer who opened the door said, "Nice to see you back, you have been missed."

I did not speak. I went to see the Chief. We shook hands and he welcomed me back. Then my whole body started to shake.

The Chief said, "I'll make you a cup of tea."

I said, "It is no good, chief. I have just got to get out of here."

The Chief then made a telephone call and a few minutes later a hospital officer arrived and escorted me to the prison hospital. The Medical Officer spoke to me he took my blood pressure and checked my pulse. The Medical Officer said, "In my opinion Mr Smith you are not fit for duty, I will arrange for you to be taken to your home and I suggest you ask your GP to come and see you. Your GP is Dr Hooper I see, I shall have a word with him if you have no objections."

I replied, "No! I must just get out of here."

The Medical Officer said, "I do understand."

I arrived home by car; my wife had been telephoned to tell her I was coming home.

Jeanie said, "Get you to bed. I half expected this to happen. I have arranged for Doctor Hooper to come and see you after he has finished his surgery."

Doctor Hooper arrived later that day. He said, "We need to talk, Mr Smith. I think it time you saw a specialist. I intend referring you to see Mr Brannon, a psychiatrist. He will be able to offer you more help than I can."

I asked, "Does this mean I am a nutcase?"

The doctor replied, "Not in the slightest."

Several weeks passed, I was feeling very ill. I could not sleep. I did not want to talk to anyone. My interests in sports, especially my fishing trips, had all come to a stop, no golf, no interest in anything; I would stay in my room doing nothing. Jean suggested it was time to visit Doctor Hooper again.

Jean made the appointment; I did not have to wait long. Doctor Hooper called to see me that same evening.

Doctor Hooper said, "I saw that you had telephoned for an appointment and as I was passing this way, I thought I would call and save you a trip to the surgery; your wife informs me you are not feeling any better."

I said, "No! I feel bloody awful. I wish I were out of it all. I am going round the bend. Why? Those tablets make me feel worse and all they do is make me sleep. I am sick of being a bloody zombie."

Doctor Hooper, whilst checking my pulse, said, "I have been discussing your problem with Mr Brannon and he thinks it would be in your best interests to go into hospital for a short time. You would only be admitted if you agree; and you would be free to leave any time you wished."

Jean said,

"I think the doctor is right, let us get you better, just like you used to be."

I said, "Well! Anything must be better than feeling like this. I will do what you want me to do."

Next day my daughter Donna called at my home; Jean had already packed all my clothes and toiletries. I kissed Jean goodbye, knowing that she would be visiting me at the hospital later that evening. I got into the car and we drove off to Whitecroft Mental Hospital.

We arrived at the hospital and I was seen by a nursing sister and shown to my room. The room was one of about a dozen, leading off a long corridor. There was a smell, not unlike the smell of a prison, urine I think they call it.

Jean came to see me that evening; later my son Duncan came to visit me. I had a feeling of helplessness; I was just like a little boy lost. The sister said my meal would be brought to my room for the next couple of days. Afterwards, I would be allowed to mix freely with the other patients; later my family left the hospital.

Later, a young nurse came to my room and said, "The night staff has taken over, my name is Sue.

If you want anything at any time just ring the bell."

I could not resist the temptation saying, "Do you mean anything? I do jest, I am a very happily married old grandfather, and I just thought it a good joke."

Christ! Was I on the mend already? That was the first time I had smiled for months.

The young nurse did not reply. She just smiled and said, "Good night Mr Smith, the alarm bell is on the right of your locker."

The nurse later brought me a drink and asked me if I wanted to have a sleeping tablet.

I replied, "Yes! I think I am going to need one; I will have a couple to make sure, if that's alright with you."

She said, "One will be enough."

I took the tablet and went out like a light.

Next day I was told to dress and was escorted to the main dining area. Breakfast consisted of cornflakes, toast and a watery cup of tea. I looked around at the other patients. There were males and females; not one of them spoke, either to me or to each other. Maybe they are all dumb, I thought!

I was hungry, so I asked the nurse for some more toast. She said, "Certainly, would you like a sausage with it?"

I said, "That would be nice."

After breakfast, the same nurse, named Vicky, said she would show me round the hospital. It was a very old hospital, yet the facilities were modern and up to date.

It looked clean, but the smell of urine never went away. After the tour, the nurse told me that a Mr Douglas would be seeing me soon. He would assess my case and decide the best form of treatment.

I did meet with Mr Douglas; he came over as a very nice man who appeared to know what the matter with me was. He asked me lots of questions and made notes.

He then said, "You will remain here for further assessment; it's a question of getting the of medication right you're, to suit your condition."

I asked, "How long will I be here?"

Mr Douglas said, "That depends on your progress, do try hard not to worry, and remember you can leave this hospital any time you want, you are a voluntary patient."

I went back to my room. Looking through the window, I could see a couple of pheasants on the lawn, a hen and a cock. I thought to myself, 'You lucky sods!' The gardens were vast and very well kept, with many large pine trees, and many other trees that I could not identify. There were birds all over the place. It was a peaceful and tranquil setting; but I was already homesick and I knew then that I could not stay here for long.

At dinner, I saw a young woman standing in a corner of the room; she was cuddling a baby in her arms. I went over to see the baby. I said, "Hello!"

The woman cowed away from me, and then she threw the baby and blanket to the floor. I was speechless! I bent to pick the baby up; to my amazement, the baby was a doll. Talk about 'One Flew over the Cuckoo's Nest' I had to get away from here. This incident had shocked me. I went to my room and telephoned Jean. There was no reply, I panicked, grabbed my coat and left the hospital by a side door. I just had to get home. I had gone about half a mile when a jeep pulled up at the side of me and two male nurses grabbed me.

One nurse said, "You may want to go home Mr Smith but that is not the way to do it, we will do it right."

I was returned to the hospital, I had the feeling of being a naughty boy. The sister met me and I was seen to my room by one of the male staff.

He said, "You did not have to run away, all you had to do was to ask to see one of the consultants who are dealing with your case; I will get you a drink of tea."

The staff was ever so kind and understanding.

Later in the day the consultant came to see me and asked, "So you do not like it here, Mr Smith? Well you can go any time that you wish."

I said, "I know you mean well, but the isolation from my wife and family is causing me a great deal of worry. I think I would prefer to go home, I would keep to the medication that you prescribed, I promise."

The consultant said, "I understand, I shall ask the sister to prepare you for discharge."

About two hours later my son Duncan arrived at the hospital. He said, "Well that was a short stay! We all thought we had got rid of you for a few weeks, at least."

I said, "That is not funny, had I remained in there I would have lost my marbles altogether."

I arrived home; Jean was so pleased to see me.

I promised her that I would keep to my medication and would never touch another drink as long as I lived. I have honoured that promise ever since.

Mental illness is one of the most dreaded illnesses there is. It can happen to anyone. Never in a million years would I have thought that I would have suffered a nervous breakdown. I am back to my normal self now, but it did take several years before the doctors found the drug that was compatible with my type of illness.

Several weeks later a welfare officer arrived at my home. She had come to inform me that because of my continual ill-health, and on the recommendation of my general practitioner and the medical officer at the Home Office, it would be in my best interest to take retirement on medical grounds.

What a way to finish twenty-five years service. I had to agree with the decision, because I did know it was in the best interests of everyone concerned; in particular for my wife, and for me. I was not the man I used to be, my confidence was at an all time low. I had been in a stressful job for far too long and it had taken its toll.

On reflection I had the option to retire when I became fifty-five. I was enjoying the job at that time, and I thought a few more years would increase my pension; how wrong I was.

There was another great shock awaiting me round the corner.

We enjoyed a very hot summer that year, and most of the family came over from the mainland to see us. We had a large house, with a very large chalet so we were able to offer accommodation to everyone, well not all at once, but they would organise their visits so they did not clash.

Jean and I would move into the chalet in the grounds of the back garden; the family would look after themselves. The older children would pitch their tents in Parkhurst Forest and they would have a ball, only returning home for their meals. I locked the car in the garage and my children would do the driving. Life was like one long holiday; bird watching, fishing and golf, eating out, what a life!

The summer and autumn seemed to pass so quickly; winter was fast moving in. On Saturday, 30 November 1990, I was watching the Benn versus Eubank boxing match, cigar in one hand and a glass of whisky in the other (back on the booze again, but only in moderation) my confidence had returned, so had my bad habits. The fight had ended and Eubank was declared the winner.

Suddenly I felt a sharp pain in my chest, pains in my neck and running down my left arm. I knew straight away that I was having a heart attack. I called to Jean who at once telephoned a doctor. Just by chance, the weekend duty doctor was driving past the end of our road. He had heard the call and was at the house inside ten minutes; by this time the pain was excruciating.

My complexion was ashen and I felt sickly. The doctor could have cut my head off for all I cared. The doctor carried out a few tests, asked a few questions and then said, "Mr Smith you are having a coronary. I shall make you feel more comfortable, an injection of morphine will ease the pain."

I then heard the sound of the ambulance siren; then all went blank.

I remember waking up. I was in hospital; I could see tubes here, there and everywhere. My mouth was dry; I asked a nurse could I have drink.

She said, "sugar and milk."

I said, "No sugar please, thanks you."

I looked at the clock on the wall; it was four o'clock.

I was wired-up to several machines; I could just see a monitor giving out all the details behind me. Across from me, on the other side, was a man in a similar position.

He was not awake and looked very pale.

I was feeling hungry, so I asked the nurse if there was anything to eat, she replied, "Eat! It is only four hours since we were fighting to save your life that is the quickest recovery I can ever remember; you can have a slice of toast at breakfast time."

I received my slice of toast. Later the consultant came to visit me and told me that I had suffered a heart attack. The next few days would be crucial; he said I was to rest.

I was in hospital for a period of ten days. I was as weak as a kitten and was very worried about the future.

I had lost a great deal of confidence and I now knew that I was not as infallible as I thought I was.

For the next nine months I was in and out of the Coronary Care Unit at least a dozen times, not actual heart attacks, but angina attacks, which give you similar symptoms to that of a coronary.

One day a consultant came to see me and said, "Mr Smith, we have decided to send you over to Southampton General Hospital, we are going to carry out some tests, including an angiogram and we will see what the computer comes up with regarding your medication requirements. It is obvious that you cannot continue having these angina attacks. You will be going to Southampton later today."

I was taken to Southampton General by ambulance. The journey took about two hours; as usual, the ferry caused the most delays.

When will islanders realise the benefits that a fixed link would bring them? On arrival at the hospital I was rushed to the theatre and prepared for the angiogram.

I was informed that I would be fully conscious throughout the whole procedure. A surgeon was on standby, in case of any complications; that was very reassuring, I must say.

I was informed that a blockage had been found and that they were going to open the blockage by inserting a small plastic bubble, angioplasty.

The operation was performed under local anaesthetic.

I could observe everything that was being done on the TV screen. I was scared, but being told earlier that a surgeon was on standby gave me more reassurance.

I returned home two days later. Although tender in certain places, I did feel much better. My pulse had a regular beat and I had more colour in my face, also my fingernails took on a pinkish hue as opposed to the purple. I was soon feeling like my old self once again.

I am now 73 years of age. It is now nearly sixteen years since that operation. I swim every day, I play golf, and my wife and I spend the winter months in the beautiful West African country of The Gambia.

I have been very lucky, but I did have to change my life style. I have never had a cigar or cigarette since my heart attack and I have had to change my diet.

Since that night in November 1900, I have had nine new grand-children and four great-grandchildren born. It is a fact I have had a new lease of life for which I am very grateful. I must thank my wife Jeanie and all my family for their love and support. Whatever the future holds, I am going to make the best of it. What a great life they have all given me.

Mother and Self: With my wonderful mother – 1983

My wife and I, in Kenya, on the occasion
of our Golden Wedding – 2002

Epilogue

I just cannot understand why most people have this obsession that the infamous Kray brothers were not the villains they actually were. Many authors make them the subject of books and films. Why? They know very well that the mention of the Krays or the Ripper will sell their products. Some writers make heroes of the infamous, like the Black Panther, the Krays and other gangland members. Most were either dead or on their deathbeds when they first met them, yet, they write as if they were on intimate terms.

I can assure you that the Krays were not the goody-goody types some writers make them out to be. They were cold-blooded killers who forced others to do most of their killing for them. They brought not only death to their victims, but terror to all those who got in their way.

You are either for the criminal or against the criminal, there is no half way. Forget the 'Robin Hood' syndrome, face up to reality, they were evil bastards.

In prison, Reginald Kray was reasonably well behaved, but this did not stop him conducting his sordid affairs from his prison cell. His dirty dealings were made for people inside and outside of the prison alike. I have spoken to Reginald Kray on many occasions, over many years. He could be kind and very courteous, but beneath this pretence was a very evil man.

These villains should not be placed on a pedestal, knock them off! They set a very bad example for our society, especially our young. The late Krays' record speaks for itself; all the Krays are now gone and the world is a much safer place. It's a shame capital punishment ended when it did. Think of it? Most of this murdering scum would have been long forgotten.

Some long-term prisoners have committed just one offence; the majority just fade into the background and get on with serving their sentences. I have a great deal of respect for these types of prisoners. On the other hand you get the ones who whinge all the time, not because they are innocent but because they cannot do their time without creating mayhem for others. To gain attention they would throw a wobbly at regular intervals. The reason? They could not do their bird.

Most of these riff-raff have had books written for them and some have even had films made about their sordid lives, some have even gone on to become TV personalities. Christ! How we scrape the barrel. If people are entertained by this hype (in most cases fictional,) so be it. Who am I to make their choice, or is it just a matter of today's society's weird priorities?

Hard Men and Jelly Babies - Dig the gist?

Addendum

I wish to add a few more details that I omitted in the book.

I wish to pay tribute to my step-father Jack (JB) Bailey who married my mother in 1952, just after Jean and I married. JB was a quiet introvert, who over the years became my mentor and a friend. JB made my mother a very happy person; she deserved happiness following her life with my real father, Fred Smith. My mother and JB enjoyed thirty-six years of happiness together; my mother died in 1988; JB lived for another ten years, but he was never quite the same after my mother died, he died in 1998 and both are still very greatly missed.

In 2006, I was contacted by a Mrs Pauline Smith who resides in Tyne and Wear. She had heard of me through Genes Re-United, this is a well-known internet web site where people can trace and seek out long lost friends and relatives. Pauline informed me that she thought that her husband Geoffrey was the son of my father, [Fred Smith], the same cruel bastard who had deserted my mother and sister in about 1945.

I telephoned Geoffrey and it was soon established that we were in fact half-brothers and that he had a sister and three other brothers – I had discovered kin that I had known nothing about. It appears that Fred Smith had two women on the go in the 1940s; in fact he fathered a child with Geoffrey's mother as early as 1942, when he was still married to my mother; when I was about nine years of age.

Discovering Geoffrey and his siblings was a big surprise, to say the least. I sent Geoffrey a copy of this book, after first warning him that I had made some adverse remarks about our father, (Fred Smith); he read the book and he informed me that Fred Smith had been the same cruel bastard with his siblings as he had been with my mother and my sister Barbara.

Geoffrey and I have become good friends and correspond regularly. I have included his family on my 'Family Tree'; after all, his kin cannot be blamed for our father's brutality. It's a very small world, and I am very pleased that I discovered my new family. Geoffrey and his wife Pauline paid us a visit in 2008, along with their young son Bret. They came over to the Isle of Wight in their camper van and stayed at a holiday park in Shanklin.

It was very nice to meet up with them and it allowed Geoff and me to catch up with the past and to reminisce, we had after all, over fifty years of catching up to do. Geoff and his family went a tour of the island with us; we had a lovely few days together. Our meeting was an event that I shall never forget. Jean said that there were a great similarity between Geoff and I, both in looks and our mannerisms, and she said she could easily see the likeness; I could see the similarities myself; although I thought I was better looking. Their son Bret was a smashing young (canny) lad and I am sure he will remember his old uncle Don for a long time to come, I hope so anyway.

In 2005 following a routine blood test PSA (Prostate Specific Antigen) and later a biopsy confirmed that I had prostate cancer. There followed thirty sessions of radiotherapy and hormone treatment, the hormone treatment lasted for eighteen months. I suffered complications; CFS (Chronic Fatigue Syndrome) and PN (Peripheral Neuropathy) to add to my troubles in 2006 I was diagnosed as having skin cancer; no doubt all that time I spent in the African sunshine; thankfully the growths were removed by a plastic surgeon and at this time it would appear to have been cured. I now have blood tests ever six months to check my PSA (Prostate Specific Antigen).

The cancer drugs were stopped after eighteen months and I gradually started to feel more like my old self; the CFS (Chronic Fatigue Syndrome) has gradually subsided and thankfully my strength is gradually returning. I still suffer from PN (Peripheral Neuropathy) which is a painful and disabling ailment, in my case affecting the lower legs and feet. I am informed that the illness will be with me for life, however, modern drugs do make life tolerable.

I was very lucky for the cancers to be diagnosed so quickly. The specialists, oncologist, radiographers and nursing staff, all played their part in my recovery. I must also thank my wife and family for their love, help and understanding. I am now in remission and have six-monthly blood tests and I must be positive in everything I do. I take things day by day; I am somewhat slower than

I used to be, however, I can now look to the future with some optimism; I thank every one of you.

All males, especially men over thirty, who have to get up for a pee several times during the night; go and consult your GP, it just may save your life. You may not have enjoyed reading my book but by following my advice above, regarding peeing, just… Remember! Take heed.

More bad news was to follow; in 2010 both my sister Barbara and her husband, who reside in Bolton, Greater Manchester, had both been sectioned and were in separate nursing homes, both are younger than me.

I was informed of this bad news by their eldest son; apparently both my sister and her husband had been ill for over a year. I had been writing and sending post cards, and I though it strange that I had never received any replies. Someone must have been reading my correspondence that I had sent to them, or my sister and her husband had destroyed them; so be it.

I could not phone them because they had gone ex-directory and had not given me their new telephone number. All cloak and dagger stuff this!

It is fair to add that Barbara and I were not on very good terms following

Some very surprising news that had I received on New Year's Eve 1998 (the same year that my step-father had passed away.) Late on that evening I received a telephone call from my sister's husband who, sarcastically, informed me that the grandfather (My mother's father) I had believed for over fifty years was in fact not my grandfather. I was livid and very angry, why, why indeed inform me of this on New Year's Eve at such a very late hour, and wait until my step father had passed away?

Albert Moore my grandfather for over fifty years, whom I was led to believe was my grandfather; who had been a regular soldier for most of his life. He was the Regimental Sergeant Major (RSM) of the Kings Own Royal Regiment; he retired with the rank of major. His wife, (my grandmother) had separated in the 1920s, they never divorced, but went their own separate ways, meeting in Bolton's town centre from time to time for a chat over a drink.

I hardly ever met Albert Moore; however, I did meet him several times and was always introduced to him as his grandson. He was always pleasant and always inquired as to my progress at school and later my apprenticeship.

Even in old age he still had that regimental appearance and military grandeur, and always sported a handlebar moustache; a very smart old man, whose brown boots were always shiny.

I tried very hard to discuss the new revelations about my new found grandfather a (Mr M) but my sister and her husband would never discuss the issue, they would slam the telephone down and eventually changed their telephone number and went ex-directory.

My mother's only living relative was her sister Edna, who resided at Netley Abbey, near to Southampton. Although in her late eighties, she had a very active mind.

I decided to go to see her and confront her regarding the mystery of my grandfather. Was Albert Moore (Her Father) my mother's father my grandfather? Who was my grandfather?

Living on the Isle of Wight I had visited my aunt Edna many time, her husband David was a likeable person, up until his retirement he had been an engineer on the liners, mostly on the Queen Mary and Queen Elizabeth. Both had been over to see my family and me on the Isle of Wight many times, and had been guests at several of my children's weddings.

I asked Aunt Edna about my granddad; she look down at the floor and said, "I thought that you may ask me that question one day, I was hoping that you would never have to ask me."

I told her what my brother-in-law had told me and she said that he was right about Albert Moore not being my mother's father, but why he had to inform me she could not understand. I asked her was (Mr M) my grandfather? "Certainly not she bawled! Your grandfather was an Anglo/Burmese man called Peter Ammed, who had a brief fling, when your grandmother and I were in Burma; I was about four years old at the time. When my mother became pregnant we sailed back to the UK so that your mother could be born here in the UK. Granddad Moore was at Maymyo, Burma at the time, training the locals on how to be soldiers; he sailed back to the UK later, but went straight on to Northern Ireland. It would be about two years before he met up with his wife and his two daughters, one of which was your mother, whom he had never seen.

He did get a shock when he first saw your mother, she was brown skinned with black her; I was a redhead just like he was. Nothing was said at the time. However, snide remarks in the sergeant's mess started the RSM to start to think, and he became very suspicious that Alice Moore [My mother] was not his daughter. It was at about this time when the marriage started to falter, and sometime later my mother and father [Your grandmother and Albert Moore] separated. RSM Moore never completely disowned your mother and was somewhat fond of her. She was a beautiful girl, lovely black hair and big brown eyes, not a pale faced, freckled, redhead like me. It is so obvious in the photograph we had taken that we could not be true sister, although we did share the same mother."

When I told my sister Barbara and her husband what my mother's sister had told me, the story was rejected out of hand and they both refused to discuss the issue? They continued to believe that a Mr M was my grandfather; I did not pursue the issue because I believed my mother's sister had told me the truth; for what reason would she make up such a story?

As I have previously mentioned my sister and her husband have far more important things to think about now. My sister has three children; I am the Godfather to two of them, I must admit that I have never fulfilled my role as a Godfather, due mainly to being many miles away from them and having six children of my own to look after. Then along came many grandchildren and great grandchildren; not an excuse, just reality.

I was last in Bolton just after my step-father died. The estate was shared equally between my sister and me. My mother had passed away ten years earlier. So I did expect a keepsake from my parent's estate; I received nothing.

In 1933 [The year I was born] my mother started keeping a diary and she made up a diary every day up until her death in 1988 – She often told me that I should have the diaries and write a book, this I had planned to do, because my mother's history, combined with that of my sister and myself would have made a very good story.

When my step father (JB) passed away I wrote many times to my sister requesting for the diaries to be sent to me, I even sent some money to cover the postage. I heard nothing for months; then one day I received a phone call from my sister informing me that she had destroyed all the diaries. What made her carry out this despicable act? Now she is in a nursing home I shall never know.

I did for some time correspond with my sister's son – He would not accept the story about his real great-grandfather. He told be many times that he had irrefutable evidence that the story of Peter Hammed was wrong. I requested that he send me this irrefutable evidence, I spoke to him on the telephone; he would not accept the version of events given to me by my mother's sister. I telephoned my sister's daughter, I left a message on the answering machine; no response; obviously they had closed ranks.

I stopped contacting them because it was obvious that they had never been told who their great-grandfather was or they had been brainwashed by their parents in believing that Mr M was their great grandfather. They feared the stigma of having a native from Burma has their great-grandfather. Did my mother know who her father was? If my mother did know, why was I never told the truth? Was my mother ashamed of who she was? I shall never know; so be it. She was a wonderful mother and grandparent, so does it matter who my grandfather was? Not to others, but it does to me.

I am now informed by the social service department [Bolton. GM] that I cannot even request information on how my sister is getting on in her new environment; I wonder if they will inform me when she passes away? My sister's siblings have certainly put the boot in.

My mother's sister's [Aunt Edna] version of events is incontrovertible, and after all it does make much more sense and does explain my mother's brown completion and big brown eyes; just like me and many of my kin.

The myths surrounding Mr M will be discussed in my next book. It should be published by next March 2012; the month of our diamond wedding; an anniversary year which we share with someone else.

Don Smith